Black Dragon Kung Fu

Advanced Training

Sifu Tony Salvitti

Copyright © 2014

Tony Salvitti

Revised edition 2017

# Contents

Introduction—5

Iron bag training—6

Sand palm—15

Hand conditioning—23

Putting out candles—32

Dragon claw—40

Iron forearms—43

Iron body—45

One finger jab—65

Training your reflexes—67

Conditioning your body—70

Primary weapons—74

Primary targets—80

Common objects as weapons—92

The law and defending yourself—94

Dit da jow formula-98

Part II Dim Mak—108

# Introduction

Black Dragon Kung Fu is literally very powerful death techniques. It is a composite system to be used only in life and death situations. This system may save your life or those you love and care about. It is not for play or to be practiced on anyone! The techniques are lethal and at the very least will cause the need for immediate medical attention to the person(s) that have had the unfortunate attempt to victimize you. One of the key reasons for having very strict rules, is because the ancient masters were well aware of the human condition and its predilection for divergent lifestyles and behavior. By setting a set of rules very strict, the student will not venture too far off the path or lose their way completely. Even if they do wander during the long years of growth towards becoming a master themselves.

If you use and apply what you have learned in this book you will walk with a new sense of confidence and power that others will notice around you. This air of supreme confidant power will be noticed by your friends and family and in fact your attackers will avoid you now and not seek you out.

# Iron bag training

Iron bag training is the end result of going through months of hard intensive training first using bags filed with mung beans, then later small pebbles, and eventually iron fillings or iron shot.

This type of training will also condition your hands and strengthen them beyond anything you have done thus far in your life. This training will increase the amount of ch'i circulating in your hands as well. However, this is only the beginning...

As with some things in nature the subtle or small becomes strong and large the longer it exists. Your life force or ch'i can also be depleted or expelled by living the wrong way (Tao) or choosing the wrong lifestyle and path.

The average person in their entire life may not even become aware of ways to cultivate the life force let alone even learn to use it and then master it. Most people just live day to day and are more concerned with the self made construct they call reality. Which is man made and try to feed its demands. It is only at the end of their life that people understand this "apparent" reality is nothing but an illusion. When one becomes a master you understand this and much more.

Hsing-I Chuan (Xingyiquan), or Mind/will- Fist, is to Kung Fu students what the alphabet is to a language. Developed by Yueh Fei, the famous general of the Sung Dynasty, and based on the principle of "force against force," this method focuses on five steps. Each step represents one of the Five Elements. The deceptive simplicity of this method makes it one of the lesser known branches of Kung Fu. But without it, a fighter will never be able to apply Chi energy in combat. Also, the system is 'linear' very similar in some respects to Karate (Ryu) used in Okinawa. Instead of the horizontal and vertical 'circular' power used in other systems of combat like; Aikido, and Tai Ch'i Chuan. There are only five basic techniques in this fighting style: crossing, pounding, crushing, drilling, and splitting. These five basic moves are sometimes referred to by the names of the five elements: earth, fire, wood, water, and metal. Beyond these basic forms, practitioners can be trained in 10 to 12 animal forms. However, these animals forms are based on the first basic five moves Xing Yi is a powerful internal art that is very useful in a combat situation. Although it still has some elements of twisting and turning like the dragon walk that are circular or elliptical in nature.

Tai Chi Chuan, or the Supreme Ultimate fist, is the second method of Internal Kung Fu. Devised to strengthen the waist, which is used as an axle in the application of Internal techniques, Tai Chi also activates the circulation of the Chi energy in the practitioner's body. Above all, Tai Chi teaches the student how to turn his body in all eight directions and how to shift his weight during each change. All the movements are done at a slow tempo which allows the practitioner to master each posture correctly and to coordinate the movements of his body with those of his arms and legs. The usage of Tai Chi techniques in combat is shown, as well as several two-man pushing hands exercises.

It is the Hsing-I Chuan and Tai chi (both internal martial arts) that served to introduce me into Black Dragon Kung Fu ( Ba gua zhang, is the third internal style of the three main Chinese martial arts. It is more broadly grouped as an internal practice (or neijia gong). Ba gua zhang literally means "eight trigram palm," referring to the trigrams of the Yijing (I Ching), one of the canons of Taoist elements of both arts are present in Black Dragon Kung Fu as well as many others. The basis of the various styles of Ba gua zhang, and the practice all styles have in common, is the circle walk. The practitioner literally walks in a circle while holding various static postures with the upper body or while executing "palm changes" (short patterns of movement or "forms" which train the body mechanics and methods of generating power which form the basis of the styles fighting techniques).

All styles have a variation of a form known as the single palm change. The single palm change is the most basic form and is the nucleus of the remaining palm changes found in the Art. Besides the single palm change, the other forms include the double palm change and the eight palm changes. The conditioning and training that are most important, for all styles is the major facet this book will cover.

One method of iron palm training requires the use of bags filled with pellets or grains of varying densities. (Mung beans or rice is used at first, followed by gravel or small pebbles, and then finally iron filings or iron shot). The student strikes these light objects at first for some months, to slowly allow the body to get used to each substance.

Training in this manner greatly decreases the chance of any long term injury from the training. Regular training is more important than progressing to the next stage.
First I will detail some of the fillings then I will tell you how you can make your own bag, you can also purchase them at martial arts supply stores.

Iron Palm-Beginning students use a canvas bag that measures approximately 10 inches by 10 inches for iron palm training. During the first phase, it is filled with mung beans, while the second and third phases call for gravel and iron balls, respectively. The students subject their hands to daily sessions of impact using four different strikes: open palm face down, open palm face up, open palm side position and claw hand. Each phase lasts three to six months, during which time the palm, the back of the hand, the side of the hand and the fingertips all undergo a hardening transformation. Arthritis is avoided by daily application of an herbal medication called Dit Da Jow.

Here is a progression of what you can fill your bag with. These are in accordance with traditional Chinese palm conditioning teachings.

In ancient days it was recommended that you spend a few months on each stage.

1) Rice, Dried Peas or Mung Beans. Anything similar.

2) Sand.   Many start at this point ( Probably best start).

3) Sand and Gravel Mix. 50/50 is good.

4) Small pebbles or Gravel. Just get what you can.

5) Steel Ball Bearing or Iron Shot.

6) Iron sand. ( Basically iron filings, the traditional final external step ).

Remember you are striking all surfaces of the hand and fist weapons, not just the palm but the difference between this method and traditional karate methods is your hand will become stronger, and tougher-without damaging it or any type of disfigurement.

This is in line with Taoist and Buddhist tradition of not mutilating the human form in anyway. Only developing it to its maximum potential without harm.

The use of a 'training bag' is not the only way to develop an extraordinary skill that you can have with you at all times. One such method is to use many layers of paper between your hand and a very hard object (stone, brick, metal) and to strike the hard object threw the paper (a phone book works or many layers of old newspapers).

You can strike the wall (if brick) for 300-1,000 times per day. Not only will this increase your toughness in your pam or fist, but increase the strength in your chest, shoulders and arms. Gradually after weeks you can reduce the amount of paper between you and the hard object you have been striking. After many more month no paper will be required and you can continue striking the hard object directly.

I myself prefer caste iron and 'used' to strike it at full power several hundred times per day. I know of one Kung Fu Master in Canada who immigrated there from China during the cultural revolution and he strikes a very thick solid steel block hundreds of times per day. His punch is so, destructive it is like getting hit with a metal hammer literally-very lethal.

But this direct method will (unlike bag training) increase callouses and calcium deposits on the striking areas of your hand the knuckles are especially vulnerable to develop greater size and density.

Back to bag training. My final 'iron palm bag' is one made of 10 pounds of steel shot, and is about 10" x 10" in size. This is in itself very useful for training as you can throw it back and forth (with or without a training partner) Or high up into the air and catch it over and over again. After a while 10 pounds will give you a workout and at the same time toughen your fingers and palm from catching it repeatedly. Combine this with proper breathing (Ch'i Kung) in a 'Ma-Bo" (horse stance) and you will have a time tested exercise to keep you busy for the next six months or more!

During this phase of your training you will also need to find a stable, strong platform to strike the 'iron pam bag' slapping it repeatedly one hand after another breathing out as you strike and inhaling as you draw up your 'iron pal'. I use a solid butchers block that is over one foot thick! If you try to use a hollow butches block eventually you will smack the 'iron palm bag' threw the one-two inches of wood. Better to use a boulder, rock, or concrete.

Remember the ch'i is what you are also trying to get to flow down and out your 'loa kun' or palm chakra you have in each of your palms. It can be achieved using just a 'mung bean bag' and not even going to sand or iron. It is the length of time you put into this training that counts not the force applied in your slapping. Compared to a person not trained in this 'kung' you will have a very distinct advantage in combat.

The reason true 'iron palm' is not demonstrated or seen on as much as it was during the turn of the century is that it does take time to develop. This is not one or two years but a true master will take up to ten years to develop and refine their skill. This is just to completely master the physical part of it. Directing the ch'i can take a lifetime.

Iron palm at this later stage can be used to heal as well as defend yourself and others. This is worth reaping the fruits of years of practice alone. Some people are naturally inclined this way and in centuries past have been known as natural healers using the 'laying on of hands' to heal the sick or wounded. Channeling the ch'i, life force, or in some religious circles 'Holy Ghost or Spirit'. All people can develop this skill, it only requires a deep seated dedication and commitment to self disciplined training.

In my opinion it is worth developing to help heal people and healing requires much more skill and power than hurting or destroying a living being.

# Sand palm

The 'sand palm' kung, is a method of chi kung that was taught to me by my late Sifu Kwan Li. I have not practiced it for very long, but I have had some very positive results from my training. It was first taught to me as a part of Black Dragon Kung Fu developed by my Sifu Kwan Li. While my primary focus in martial arts has been the internal styles of Tai Ch'i Chuan and Hsing-I Chuan, this was given to me to supplement my training. Specifically, it is a very structured process whereby one helps open the meridians to allow chi to pass freely. This, in turn, helps one develop proper structure and a deeper level of relaxation, and self discipline.

But before the training begins a note on effective fighting techniques. When fighting a larger enemy, specifically on that has a reach advantage and height. This should automatically set your training and power to direct it at the opponents limbs, (hands, forearms, arms, feet, and legs). This is what will be thrown at you or reaching to grasp you. If you try to go inside towards the larger opponents body. You will be at a severe disadvantage and get attacked. You must maintain a 'cool head' and think first before you act. Distance yourself, then if a fist or hand is thrown strike it with all your might, twist the fingers, punch the firearm, tie up the legs. Once your opponent has no limbs they will be as helpless as a baby.  I have seen too many fighters rush in, and get destroyed because they did not 'size up' the opponent objectively. Granted this is not always possible as in ambushed, or sudden assaults on the street. This is why many years of practice in the dojo, kwoon, or dojang. Is needed so you can be able to make snap decisions and become the victor instead of the victim!

Sand Palm (also; yellow, red, and black and sand palm) named as such, not because its practitioners can make their own palm red, rather due to the mark that is left on the opponent that they strike. The power generated as a result of this training is, like any internal martial art, subtle yet devastating. Many people in China are familiar with the name Red Palm, but are not aware of the depth of the Art. What I will detail later in this article is the first level of Sand Palm kung. Some systems of Pa Kua use this to increase the power of their strikes. This works and is great training to get the chi to flow stronger to the hands and feet. But, what fewer people know is that, in fact, there are nine levels to this training. The first three levels are referred to as tiger. The second three levels are referred to as dragon. The last three are tiger and dragon. There is no way to rush the training process. Each level requires the student to achieve a certain level of chi flow, either in or out, before he can progress to the next level. To hurry the process would be a waste of time and yield nothing.

The benefits of studying Sand Palm are many. This practice will help the mind focus more clearly. Also, the feeling of chi that one develops will come rather quickly as compared to other methods. These feelings may vary some between individuals, but they are real and not the product of mere imagination. This method of training is excellent for building chi to improve ones health and one's martial abilities. At higher levels of development, the student will imagine that his/her body has the clarity of crystal due to the exchange of chi between the person and the environment. After a while, the student will naturally be able to absorb chi as well. This absorption is not an abstract conception or a form of visualization. It is real and can be felt as well as demonstrated at higher levels. This also helps to build chi. Later, one can consciously move chi within the body. This direction comes from the mind and can actually be felt within. Eventually, one will develop the ability to project chi outside the body Kong Jin). This can have great health/healing benefits as well as martial application. The body itself will also benefit from this method of training. The chi will fill the body and energize it. Your hair will become stronger and brighter. Finger nails will become stronger (and grow faster). The muscles and ligaments will grow in strength and elasticity. The bones will strengthen and harden. The circulation within the internal organs will improve leading to better health. These are but a few of the benefits to be had from practicing Sand Palm.

To begin the first level of training, one should be comfortable in wuji. The purpose of wuji is to calm the mind and to allow the natural structure of the body to settle and release tension. This has the effect of calming both the mind and the body. Properly done, the ch'i will flow freely throughout the body and gather in the tan tien. Initially, one must stand with the feet about shoulder width apart (Ma-Bo or horse riding stance). The weight should focus on the bubbling well. There are three points which should be aligned. The bubbling well of the feet; imagine a line connecting the two. The huyin which is a point between the anus and the genitals. And the bai hui which in near the crown of the head. To accomplish this, the head will be tilted slightly forward and it will feel as if you are leaning a bit too far forward. The tongue should be lightly pressing the roof of the mouth, just behind the front teeth. Close your eyes and relax imagining the tension leaving your body. Start from the head and go down. I practice wuji for a few minutes prior to beginning the first level.

After calming the mind and body in wuji for a few minutes, move your hands so that the palms face the ground. Keep your arms at your sides, just rotate the palms so that they face the ground. Take care not to stiffen the wrist while doing this. From here, exhale and lightly increase the pressure of the tongue to the roof of the mouth and lightly press your teeth together as you relax and imagine the chi going from the tan tien to the palms while the ten toes grasp the ground and two eyes stare forward. As you inhale, simply relax and breathe deeply into the tan tien. Keep the mind free and remember to watch your structure. Repeat this nine times.

For each palm position, repeat the exercise the same way. For the next position, raise and extend your arms so that the palms are facing away from you at shoulder height. Keep the elbows pointing down and relax the shoulders. Perform the exercise as mentioned above for nine repetitions.

The third position requires the student to stretch the arms out to each side at shoulder height so that the palms are facing away to the sides with fingers pointed upwards. Perform the exercise as mentioned above for nine repetitions.

To do the exercise in the fourth palm position, raise the hands above the head to about 45 degrees from vertical. Raise your head so that you are looking at the space between the palms. Turn the palms slightly inward and extend the arms. Perform the exercise as mentioned above for nine repetitions.

After practicing for a period of time, if you feel comfortable, you can clench the teeth harder, increase the number of repetitions not to exceed 36, and push harder.

While it seems like the exercise detailed above is simple, it is profound in its results if practiced correctly and consistently. Eventually, one would increase the repetitions and corrections would be made as required. These are the basic exercises of the first level of Sand Palm kung. Many internal martial artists and chi kung practitioners have performed this level and achieved excellent results in improved chi flow to the hands and feet as well as increasing ones striking power. For most this is enough. But, this is really only scratching the surface of this Art for there are actually nine levels. I have personally benefitted from practice and so have many members of my dojo, kwoon, or dojang who have been instructed in this to improve circulation. I hope that some of you will try this exercise for a few months and receive the benefits that it has to offer.

After som time you may experience various new sensations both in mind and body. While you become more familiar with the enhanced movement of ch'i in and around your body. This can be accompanied by physical, and auditory, and visual phenomena not to worry. It will pass in time or you can even control it by focusing your will power.

You do understand that where the "will" goes the mind and body follows in that specific order. By increasing your ch'i and thereby increasing your own bodies frequency. You can develop "ding jing" or static repelling energy. When you are relaxed standing you can actually make a person, animal, or object move back away from you or attract and move toward you. This phenomena happened to me when a Tae Kwoon Do friend of mine Bob, felt this energy push him back away from me and against a wall. To this day Bob cannot explain how he was pushed back.

# Hand conditioning

Traditional methods of conditioning the hands and fingers have spread all over Asia. It was in Japan that I learned this method for 'conditioning' the hands into a much more tougher weapon. Most farmer's and hard working people already have a tougher than average skin, and thickness. If you are already a hard worker you know this is a fact.

If you have soft delicate skin and need it to be more rugged depending on how often and the beginning or advanced level your hands will develop in strength as well.

To begin get a large wooden box or 5 gallon bucket and fill it 3/4 full of uncooked rice. Then every morning or every evening (the time is not critical just keep a regular time) start thrusting your hands one after another deep into the rice. If you want to count the thrusts you will need to do about 200-300 times per hand. Or just put on some good music and go at it until exhausted. Remember to inhale as you draw back your hand and exhale as you thrust deeply into the rice. The repeated contact with the rice will over days and weeks make your skin adapt and it will become more durable than before training.

After each session of thrusting your hands in and out of the rice bucket. Alternately grab a handful of the rice and attempt to crush it. Then take handfuls and in a rubbing motion between both palms squeeze and attempt to pulverize the rice into powder.

The need to go to stage two of this type of conditioning is entirely up to you. Replace the rice with sifted sand (make sure no foreign objects are in the sand as you could injure yourself thrusting your hand into it. Repeat the training process again for another three months and your hands will now be even stronger and tougher than before.

To proceed to stage three is even more drastic but your hands after this training period will become very deadly weapons. Replace the sand with small gravel and repeat the process your should have now become adept at doing even in your sleep.

After this training your skin and hands will be very rugged, calloused, and strong. One should stretch your hands and fingers and massage them thoroughly to avoid stiffness and inflexibility. You should do this for 3 months (or longer if you wish). After every training session wash your hands and then apply a good lotion or oil (olive oil, or peanut oil is excellent) to the skin let it absorb and dry (this is why it is good to do every night before you go to sleep). Also, always after every type of training stretch out the body parts being trained-this includes legs (after kicking) arms (after punching), back and chest (after bodybuilding), etc.

Remember, training is not recommended at all for those under 16 years of age. Those individuals under 18 years of age must get permission from a parent or guardian before starting training. Always consult a physician before beginning any exercise program.

The iron palm method is the hand conditioning regimen that I prefer. I enjoy the set schedule for training, the relaxed method, and most of all, the speedy results. I also prefer this method because it trains the palm heart, or the flat of the palm. In my opinion, the flat palm slap is the trademark strike of fighting gung fu. Iron palm is the essence of the gung fu of legend, not the watered down version that so many modern practitioners bring to fights, only to be crushed.

There is no mistaking an iron palm slap for boxing, karate, or mindless street brawling. As for its application in tamashiwari, the iron palm is unrivaled when it comes to breaking solid objects. Though you might be inclined to think otherwise, it is much easier to break a brick with the iron palm than it is with a punch, chop, hammer-fist, or palm heel strike. I know this from experience. Iron palm is also noted for its capability of breaking the bottom brick in a stack without spacers. Such a practice is known as selective breaking.

My Sifu Kwan Li, was a master of the of the iron palm, and could break bricks selectively in a stack. Iron palm falls short only when it comes to breaking flexible objects (wood, baseball bats) and objects with spacers. I explain it to people with this example- the palm slap can move anything it strikes one half an inch. Since cement cannot flex, it breaks. If the object, such as wood, can flex farther than that, it will not break. This is only an exaggerated example mind you, and only an example of my personal theory at that. As for spacers, the palm has difficulty sending energy through "hollow" area.

There are many variations of the iron palm conditioning process and each usually has a set amount of time for the initial phase. During this first phase, training must be done daily. After that, maintenance training varies. The first phase ranges anywhere from one month to three years or more. There are also advanced levels of the iron palm as well as internal and external conditioning.

The regimen I use is a variation of the traditional 100 day method and combines both internal and external training. This method produced good results for me in minimal time. Many others have also reported favorable results. I will honestly tell you that 100 days is not enough time to produce an invincible palm, but it will create a hand that is dangerous enough for combat, as well as allow you to break red bricks. This regimen conditions the entire hand.

Train at your own pace and exercise caption with good common sense.

Materials Needed:

1) 10" wide x 24" long (or larger) canvas bag

2) approx. 1" round river rocks (enough to fill the bag half way)

3) old towel

4) cinder blocks (support stand)

5) dit da jow, or massage oil (olive, peanut).

The method is as follows:

Set up the cinder blocks so that you can sit on one and the other(s) create a stand in front of you that is about the height of your naval (while seated). If the surface of your stand is not level due to the shape of the cinder block, you may have to lay an additional concrete slab on the top for a nice flat surface. Place the towel (in single layer) over the support stand. This is your striking surface.

Fill the canvas bag with the rocks and fold the remaining half of the bag over to create a side that is double layered. Tape the bag shut (masking or duct tape will do). Place the bag on the stand and your simple setup is complete.

*When striking for training, it is important to stay relaxed and allow your hand to drop onto the surface. This should be accompanied with a exhalation breath and in halation per each slap of the bag. This means 200-300 times per hand! Which has a daily cumulative training effect on its own.

Do not tense the arm or shoulder, or exert strength while striking. Always breath out as you strike. Exerting strength or failing to breath out is said to stress the heart. This has affected some individuals over the years and is something to keep in the back of your mind, while training.

1) Drop your flat palm on the bag 30 times, shake out the hand, strike another 20 times, shake out the hand and flex.

2) Drop your knife hand on the bag 30 times, shake, 20 times, shake and flex.

3) Repeat for the palm heel surface.

4) Repeat for the back of the hand.

Now remove the bag so that you are now striking the cement/cinder support covered with the towel.

1) Drop your knife hand 30 times, shake, 20 times, shake and flex.

2) Repeat with the palm heel.

3) Repeat with the flat palm.

4) (optional) Strike with back-fist 30 times and repeat with straight fist.

5) This can also be used to give yourself "iron elbows". Repeated downward strikes will gradually build up and strengthen your already natural weapons.

Additional training:

You can supplement with a bucket of sand. Straight punch the sand 30 times and repeat with the back-fist. Do 100 spear-hand thrusts into the sand. You can also rub the sand between you hands to toughen the skin.

Some iron palm practitioners feel that it is unwise to train the knuckles of the fist because of possible long term joint damage. This is fine for strict iron palm fighters, but if you train in any fist striking art, it may be wise to strengthen your knuckles. Chinese acupressure teaches that training the fingertips can weaken the eyes. Take this into consideration when training spear-hand but also realize that plenty of karate stylists train fingertips and can see just fine.

Different teachers advocate different numbers of strikes per session. Some use hundreds or even thousands of repetitions. Some say to train three times a day, others say you must train the exact same time everyday without missing a day. Maybe these routines are ideal, but with the method I outlined above, you can train whenever and even miss a day or two. The less days you miss, the better it will be for you. You should achieve impressive results after 100 days of training. At that point, you should be able to break a single patio block with a flat palm slap (use a towel padding at first).

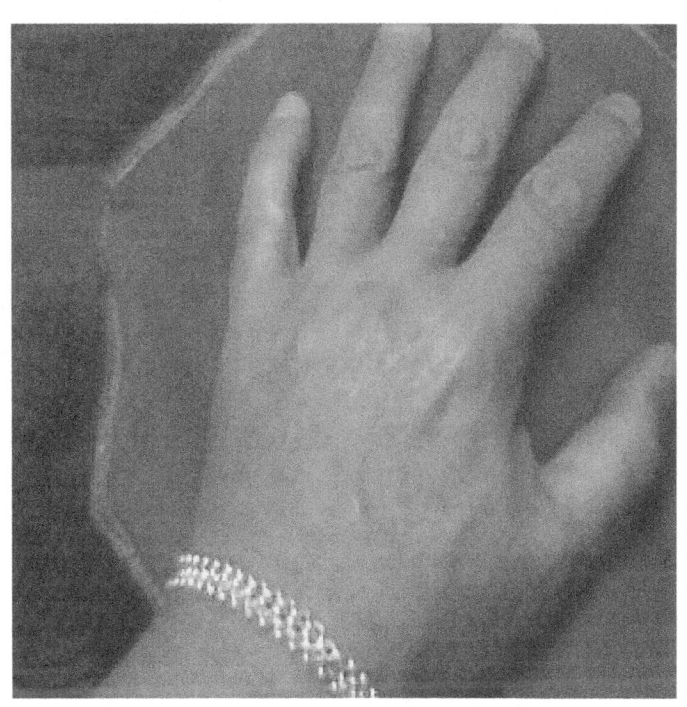

# Putting out candles

After conditioning you may wish to concentrate on that most amazing ability... Speed! Not just fast but super fast reflexes that will literally blind your opponent before he can make a move to block a punch. Or as in the case of the late Bruce Lee, (who know doubt was a very fast martial artist). But his 'attempted punches' were in fact blocked by an equally (if not faster) opponent Grand Master Victor Moore. This was filmed at the Bruce Lee vs Vic Moore (Demo & Sparring, 1967 Int. Karate Tournament) . So, the fast speed can be used to block a enemy that has fast reflexes as well.

I have spoken to Victor Moore about this and a lot of the video footage is skewed to only showing Bruce Lee without showing the blocks I have seen (if you research further) and eyewitness testimonies do indeed state that Bruce Lee's punches were blocked by Victor Moore.

With that said and done. How to increase your speed will depend on when you start training. Both Victor Moore and Brice Lee, started training in body athletic endeavors and martial arts at a young age (Victor Moore,,started even younger than Bruce Lee at age 6 while Lee was 12-14 years old).

The younger you start training your nervous system the better. You will have a huge advantage over a 'couch potato' that only has a lame job and comes home and plays video games. If you only did regular athletic training compared to these 'couch potatoes' you would seem like superman. But that is what we are after advanced flash-like blinding speed! The ability to end a fight as soon as it begins. Mere seconds are all that a fight should take-never minutes and the longer a fight goes on the greater risk you have of losing.

Without getting too much into human physiology. What you are going to do is build or train your body to react before you can even think to throw a punch or kick or block an enemy or dodge out of the way. This is known as constructing a 'reflex arc'.

When you move certain ways and do so over, and over again many thousands of times. Your nervous system will develop and you will actually develop new nerve connections and after a time these connections become small ganglions (nerve clusters) that act as small brains. You actually already have a huge second brain in your 'solar plexus' this large ganglion keeps you breathing automatically and if you have been punched or kicked there your 'solar plexus' is temporarily stunned and you get your breath knock out of you.

Similarly you can create certain movements by repeated motion and concentration it will require time and it is worth the effort put forth because once the training is done and the new nerve 'reflex arc' created it will stay with you a lot longer than your built up muscles. To begin this type of training you will need regularity in your training everyday at the same time-set it aside just for your blinding speed training.

To go along with this training you will need control and agility. Just throwing a fast punch and kick is good, but you have to be able to hit a moving target.

Get a length of rope, or wire that you can attach a tennis ball to and hang it from a height that the target (tennis ball) will be at. If you wish to practice at striking the head make it dangle from five to six feet. If you want to practice the chest or abdominal area hang it lower. You should be able to swing the ball freely and then observe and throw punches or kicks at hit and see how many times you can hit it. This is not the speed part of your training however, it will also help with this too. Use that exercise as a warm up for your super-fast training which you will begin next light a good size candle and take a step back allow approximately six inches to one foot away from the lit flame from either your extended fist, palm or foot (if practicing for kicks). Now very carefully extend your fastest punch at the flame exhaling as you You are going to be putting this candle out by the speed of your moving limb without touching it directly!

Again place the candle on a stable platform or table in the area you will be making the repeated strikes with your hands or feet. If you are practicing a side kick, front kick or roundhouse the candle should be just out of your foots final extended position. If you are practicing forward thrust punch or side to the head or chest level them place the candle slightly below the area you would strike normally. This gives you ample time to slightly squat down into a stance and begin repeated strikes out to the candle. Note the flame will flutter and depending on your return speed want to follow you hand.

Do not be discouraged if you cannot make the candle flame dance just yet. Repeated practice will give you results. The foundation you lay down now will last a lifetime. Do not cheat yourself out of a once in a lifetime chance to develop a real super-power.

You may be familiar with the saying; "The hand is quicker than the eye." This is very true and to add to that the 'untrained eye'. If you have noticed after playing with a baseball at times you can see the ball traveling as it turns and while it may have been not noticed by the onlookers in the stands because you are 'in the game' your sphere of focus is more intense and you can see things more clearly and because of your eye muscles have been tracking fast moving objects you can now see motion not usually identified by people.

This is how your can train your eyes, in a similar manner. Get a fist sized ball or even a rock. Get into a horse stance (Ma-Bo) and then begin tossing the rock or ball up in front of you. But unlike a juggling act, you are using only one object. I want you to catch the rock or ball with an overhand grip grab and thrust down motion.

This will serve to increase your grip reflex you have to be pretty fast and strong to grasp an object palm down and then re-launch it back out in front of you or straight up into the air above you and catch it with your other hand. Repeat this exercise while watching the object and soon you will be able to see the object turning in slow motion. It takes time and dedication but it will happen.

After six months or more of this type of training you will be able to see faster moving objects such as arrows flying or a coin tossed into the air. While these mundane things may seem pointless, the benefits will be that you will now see a punch or and kick or strike coming at you and have the advantage of speed of sight. This gives you time to react either move out of the way or intercept the fist, elbow, or foot. Counter it and attack it directly or redirect the energy and send them flying or tie them up in a lock or hold.

Lets get back to the candle now. You should be practicing the strike you want to make your fastest and this should take you anywhere from 20-30 minutes of non-stop high velocity strikes.

Increase the distance between you and the candle after you are able to put it out with just the kick or punch you are able to do at first perhaps just back away one foot. Begin training and you should be well on your way to increased speed. In fact by now you should be able to gauge your speed as much faster than before.

A good tip is to always be relaxed. If you are too tense this will slow down your reflex and if you are too relaxed it will also imped your speed. Inhale and then exhale with a resounding snap and like a good billiard player put some English on the ball. You want to put that same snap into your target or enemy.

This is where kung fu differs from regular boxing or external arts. When you are hit with regular punch or kick it is like a wood or iron beam hitting you. But when you are hit by a martial artist especially an 'internal martial artist'. It is like getting hit with a iron ball attached to a chain and being swung at you very hard. The surface damage to you is not that great but the internal damage done can be devastating and even kill you.

Some people have had exploded spleen's (ruptured due to a 'iron palm' slap). This may result in a slow bleed and over the course of days the person that was struck may think nothing is seriously wrong. Internally the spleen's membrane could be bleeding into the abdominal cavity and death could be hours or days away. This is why you should dodge out of strikes to your body and never underestimate your aggressor.

Anyway, by this time your should be able to hit a enemy several times per second! Using both hands and have developed a lot of stamina from the daily practice of speed punching or kicking.

A lot of ancient legends are built on some truth and over time things are added to the tales. This is in all cultures and many types of genres, not just martial arts. So, when you hear of people putting out candles from many feet away. Take it with a grain of salt and always use good common sense and objectivity.

To be sure you will develop your reflexes fast and increase your accuracy, speed, and stamina. What you do with your new ability will determine one of the many paths you will follow in life. Always keep in mind "right thought equals right action".

# Dragon claw

Dragon claw 'kung' is similar in some respects to the other styles of claw kungs; Eagle, Mantis, and Tiger. However, this training will transform your hands in to excellent defensive and offensive weapons. No long tales here just a plain and simple fact. In fact the longer you practice this dragon claw kung training the more powerful you will become. Every time you grasp an enemy, they will feel searing pain .

By now you should be aware of correct breathing methods and the importance of good developed abdominal muscles. "Breath is the lord of strength". You are only as strong as your internal structure will allow. The development of true strength begins with the internal organs and in this case your lungs.

So, before you even get to train your "Dragon claws" you must first (everyday) do one hundred sit-ups and one hundred leg raises. Followed by standing in a Mo-Bo or horse stance and do some light to moderate deep breathing and ch'i kung*. After this warm-up every day during the morning hours are best. I get up personally at 3 AM every morning as this is the hour of the lungs.

*See my book "Secrets of ch'i kung" for more information on this subject.

You will need to obtain a few things to begin your training;

1) A fist size amount of modeling clay.

2) A large mouth glass or ceramic jar that hold 3-5 gallons. (Or a 5 gallon bucket with an attached dowel).

3) Oil or dit da jow.


Dragon claw kung, will make your hands into an awesome controlling power. When you grab an enemy they will feel pain all the way to the bone.

Obtain a 5 gallon bucket, then attach a 2-3 inch long wooden dowel or handle. Mount it vertically so you have to grasp it with just your fingers and thumb, when picking it up. Or a glass or kiln fired pot with a small neck and mouth, will work just as well.  Practice grasping and raising the bucket or your jar with just your fingers and thumb of each hand, breathing in as you lower the training device, exhaling out as you raise it to chest level. Now everyday add one bowl of water into your bucket or jar. Do this for about 15 minute's non-stop with each hand.

After only a few months the strength in your hands should have tripled (by now the bucket or jar should be filled with water). Now you are ready for the next step, empty all the water out and start to add a bowl of sand every day until the bucket or jar is full again.

Then once again empty the sand out of the bucket or jar, and add a bowl full of iron or lead shot (lead can be used because you are not actually touching it just using it for weight). After you can pick up the bucket or jar now full of metal the yang half of the dragon's claw will be complete. Also, during the day when you are watching a show or reading. Grasp the modeling clay and squeeze it in every way you can think of an alternate to the other hand. This is something you can do and it will serve to strengthen the nerve force even more increasing your gripping power.

Then begin the yin part of training. Every night for at least 15 minutes each hand. Practice your dragon claw, by pointing your fingers and thumb at the moon. Try to grasp the distant object and extend your ch'i to it. After this is done each night your should massage each hand with the other use the oil (olive or peanut oil) and or some dit da jow. This will relax your hands so you can get a good nights sleep.

This type of griping practice will bring the ch'i into the fingers. At this point you should be able to control any animal or man, by your dragon claws alone.

# Iron forearms

Iron forearm kung, is one of the faster ways to develop an extraordinary power. First find a suitable tree in a field, or a deeply buried round wooden post (I am fortunate enough to have two trees that are growing a few feet from each other to train on in my back yard) . Stand in a horse riding stance (ma bo). Every day at the same time, for about 15-20 minutes exhale out as you alternately slap your inner and outer forearms against it.

After you do this be sure to massage each of your forearms. In six short months, your forearms will have become a lot harder to the touch and a lot stronger.

Now find a large rock or boulder, that does not have jagged or sharp edges, now at the same time everyday start hitting your inner and outer forearms against the rock, breathing in when pulling away and exhaling, when you strike the rock. After six months, your firearms will now be like iron. You can use them to strike or block any blow.

Additional grip strength can be obtained by the following: Get a bucket or wooden box of sand, filled to about a foot deep.

Take both hands and scoop up the sand. Press both hands together exhaling at the same time. Flex your chest muscles and try to crush the sand into dust. Do this every day, or every other day, until your forearms are pumped with blood.   Then take a wrist roller, or make one. Take a wooden dowel about 12 inches long, 1-3 inches thick. Drill a hole in the center, and attach a thick cord. On the other end of the cord attach a weight 3-10 lbs.

Now again stand in the "ma-bo" stance and holding the dowel with both hands, raise it to chest level. Now start to twist and turn the dowel, as you do the weight will come up off the ground wrapping around the middle of the dowel, until the weight is at chest level. Then reverse the motion and unwind the weight back down to the ground. Keep doing this until you are exhausted and can no longer move it. This is done as a nonstop exercise to also increase your stamina.

That is it, now you should have extraordinary strength in your grip hand strength, and hardness in your forearms.

# Iron body

## (Jinzhong zhao or Gold bell cover)

The iron body is acquired by certain well defined training techniques that include breathing, exercises, abstention from sex, meditation, and a very intense or focused concentration. The student learns to flow and direct his ch'i to permeate his muscles with such hardness that no foreign objects can penetrate. Not only resistant to punctures, the body is also protected against lacerations, abrasions, and bruises.

This is the key to the iron body: breathing and the associated isometric contraction that tenses and hardens all the muscles of the body. Once in this state, the only way an enemy may defeat you is to disturb your breathing or concentration. Correct breathing is one of the foundations of the iron body. Ch'i kung breathing involves both correct abdominal breathing, all sides of the abdominal wall must be uniformly expanded like a balloon when air is taken in. At the same time the diaphragm must be kept relaxed and down. I cannot stress enough the importance of mastering breathing and regular abdominal contractions. This can be done while sitting in a car, or a chair, even standing in a lone waiting. This is often forgotten and should be practiced regularly. My own training at times has become lax due to other matters in life and I did for a time 'forget' to do the breathing exercises and abdominal contractions. A lot of older martial artists and athletes in general. As one gets middle age become wound-down and not as active. This is one of the reasons excess fat accumulates over the abdominal areas that in the younger years were lean and healthy.

Reverse abdominal breathing involves contracting the abdominal wall, keeping the diaphragm down and staying relaxed as air is inhaled. Exhalation is just the reverse of inhalation in both correct and reverse abdominal breathing.

The chest is not collapsed or raised (as in military attention stance) having a flat lumbar region, knees bent and both feet firmly placed on the ground.

The next step is the micro-orbit. This orbit consists of two meridians a back one (governor) and a front one (conception), along which ch'i flows.

The governor channel starts at the perineum, midway between the anus and the genitals, and follows the spine to the crown of the head and ends at the palate.

The conception channel begins at the tongue and travels down the center of the body to the perineum. These two channels must be connected by placing the tongue on the roof of the mouth. This creates a closed loop circuit which your ch'i will flow.  Real iron body training begins after you have cultivated and nourished your ch'i which can be circulated to the organs and their protective tissues. This is achieved by combining both correct and reverse abdominal breathing with contractions of various inner body musculatures. The next step is to condition the body to accept strikes without resulting in injury. This conditioning, when combined with ch'i makes the body impervious to injury.

Iron hand and iron body skills have always intrigued me and I'm not alone. You can find quite a few articles on the subject and there are more than a few people selling books, videos, and courses on the subject. The idea of developing bone crushing power and the ability to take the most power strikes your opponent can muster is always going to be compelling for the martial artist. However, I've found that until now there all that has been available are routines that are either too conservative in their approach, too extreme, or simply provide an incomplete picture of iron skills training. In terms of this training I've had hands on instruction, bought books, bought videos, and even attended seminars. I've practiced what I learned for nearly ten years now. Over the years I've mixed routines, added drills and exercises, and dropped things out completely. What I now practice and teach is, I feel, the most effective and efficient method of iron skill development you will come across. The method presented in the following pages is the basic level of iron skill development. Higher level development includes more advance internal power development exercises. However, what you will find in this book is much more advanced than most other information on the iron skills.

I feel that a complete course in the development of the Iron Skills should involve considerable conditioning of the following aspects of the marital artist:

1) The mind and internal Energy - this can be accomplished through the use of Ch'i-kung, internal power exercises (nei jing gong), and the proper use of focus (intent and will).

2) The musculature - This can be accomplished through the use of specific physical bodybuilding type exercises.

3) The skeletal structure and skin - This can be accomplished through specific types of impact training.

My method of Iron Skills development includes all three of these aspects. In the following piece I will describe in detail the esoteric martial arts approach to Iron Skills Development, I include all the basic drills and exercises for the development of basic level iron hand and iron body as well as a discussion on how to set up a routine to get the most out of your training. The following pages will detail the way you can set up and train on a regular basis. Please feel free to omit or add your own best suited training exercises that you are getting the best results with. By all means if a particular exercise or training method is not working for you-omit it. You will find that some methods work better than others and as always experience is the best teacher.

Ch'i kung:

1) Open and Close the Gate Ch'i kung - Begin standing up, spine neutral, and with your feet should width apart. Your arms should be held out in front of you at chest level. Your palms should face each other and be about a foot apart. Place your tongue to the roof of your mouth. You will be breathing in and out of your nose in the Taoist way for both of these Ch'i kung.

First, place your attention on the back of each hand. You should be able to feel the back of your hands with your mind. Inhale and begin to open your arms as though you are about to give someone a huge hug. You will open your arms fully until you are in a cruciform position. At this point you will begin to exhale, reverse the movement, and switch you attention to your palm as you begin to close your arms. Once your hands are about six inches to one foot apart you will to inhale and, once again, place your attention onto the backs of your hands. This time, however, instead of opening your arms you will turn your palms so that they face away from you and you will be drawing your hands in towards your chest. Make sure to keep your elbows down as you do this. When your hands reach about six inches away from your chest you will reverse this movement. Remember to coordinate this final movement with you exhalation and to place you attention on your palms. When you have returned to the starting position you will have completed one repetition of this Ch'i kung. You will need to complete a total of nine before moving on.

Remember to always coordinate your physical movements with your breathing and stay relaxed. You will place you attention on the backs of your hands as you open your arms and as you draw your hands to your chest. You will place your attention on your palms as you close your arms and as you push out with your hands. Doing this will lead your ch'i (internal energy) to those areas which is a vital ability for later exercises.

2) Gathering Clouds Ch'i kung - Begin standing up, spine neutral, and with your feet shoulder width apart. Your arms will hang loosely at your sides. Place your tongue to the roof of your mouth. Your breathing will be the same as in the first Ch'i kung.

Start by inhaling and raising your arms up towards the sky in an arching motion with your palms facing up. Continue this movement until your arms are overhead and your palms are facing each other - they should be about six inches apart. As you begin to exhale turn your palms downward to face the ground and move your palms along a downward path towards your groin area. You will keep your hands close to each other and close to your body as you do this. Once your hands reach your groin area you have completed one repetition of this Ch'i kung. You will need to complete a total of nine repetitions before moving on to other exercises.

Muscle Strengthening:

Static Core Work: The following drills, of holding static postures for periods of time, will greatly strengthen your body - especially your core. While you hold these postures remember to breathe through your nose with your tongue held to the roof of your mouth and utilize the Taoist breathing method.

1) Floor Plank - Begin lying on the floor on your stomach. Your forearms will be under you and you will press up as though doing a pushup except all of your weight is on your forearms not your hands. You will maintain this static position for as long as possible, but your goal should be one minute. You can work up to more than one minute but anything more and a minute and a half won't be necessary. I'll explain further in the building a routine section.

A) Ball Plank: You can make this exercise more difficult by using one of those huge abdominal balls. Simply place you feet on the ball or place your forearms on the ball. To make it really difficult you can attempt to suspend yourself between a chair and a ball (feet on chair, forearms on ball) or between two balls.

B) Side Plank: Another variation I like to throw into my routine is the side plank. In this variation you will begin by lying on your side with your feet on top of each other. You will use one forearm to support yourself. Don't let you hips sag down. This will really strengthen you oblique muscles. Thirty seconds on each side is a good goal time.

2) Iron Bridge - You will need two chairs (or wooden boxes) for this exercise. You will suspend yourself between the two chairs. Place your feet on one chair and place your upper back and head on the other. Use only the muscles necessary to keep yourself straight - no sagging! As you get stronger move the chairs further and further apart until you are suspended between the two with only your feet and head. You can further increase the difficulty by resting small weight plates on your lower abdomen. Start slow and don't increase the weight too soon! Your goal is one minute.

3) San Shou Bridge - This form of the Bridge is similar to a Wrestler's Bridge. You begin by lying on your back with you knees bent, feet flat on the floor, and your hands near your ears. You may need a towel or small pillow for your head. From this position lift

yourself up so that your weight is supported between your feet and your head/hands. You body will form an arch. While holding this position you can do some rocking and attempt to touch your nose to the floor. As your strength and flexibility increase you will be able to do it. Again strive to reach the one minute mark.

4) Front Bridge - Start doing the bridge on a consistent basis should spend some time in the Front Bridge as well. Start by lying on your stomach with your feet spread apart and your hands near your head. Lift your body off the floor so that you are supported by only your feet and head/hands. Make sure you touch your chin to your chest. Hold this position for one minute.

You can perform this series of exercises in circuit fashion. You should strive to hold the positions for 1 minute to one and half minutes. You can rest anywhere from 30 seconds to one minute between positions. When you become more advanced you can move through each position with no rest between them. You only need to complete one circuit of these exercises.

Dynamic Strengthening:

1) Abdominal Wheel - You will need to pick up an ab wheel from your local fitness retailer. To use it start by kneeling on the floor (you may need a pillow for your knees) and holding the ab wheel by the handles. The wheel should be on the floor and near your legs. Keep you core tight and push forward on the wheel to roll out. Your goal is to reach out as far as you can so that your body is just hovering over the floor. Then reverse the movement and return to the starting position. Inhale as you roll out; exhale as you return to the starting position. Work up to being able to complete multiple sets of 10-25 repetitions.

2) Twisting - Stand holding a weight (I prefer a medicine ball, but a dumbbell or some other weight will work as well) straight out in front of you and keep you feet should width apart. Begin twisting your upper body to the left and right at a fairly quick pace. You can also vary the angle of your twists for a more complete development.

3) Side Bends - Stand with your feet shoulder width apart and your arms above your head and simply bend side to side. You can make this exercise more difficult by holding a weight in your hands. At first a weight as little as 2lbs will be sufficient. Start small and work your way up slowly.

4.) Fingertip and Knuckle pushups - You will need to do pushups on both your knuckles and your finger tips to strengthen the muscles, tendons, and ligaments in your forearms and hands. When doing knuckle pushups you will place you weight on the last three knuckles. When doing fingertip pushups you need to make sure you keep your fingers bent in a claw shape. Attempting to keep them too straight will result in poor conditioning. Also do not allow your fingers to bend backwards as this will result in unsatisfactory conditioning. It may be very difficult to complete a proper fingertip pushups at first. You can progress from static holds in the kneeling pushup position, to kneeling fingertip pushups, and finally progress to full fingertip pushups.

5) Pushing and Pulling Iron Block - Begin by standing with your feet wider than shoulder width apart and knees bent. You will start with your hands near your armpits and palms facing outward. Inhale and tense all of the muscles in your body. As you exhale press your hands forward as though you are pushing a huge iron weight. Once you fully press out your arms (but, not to lockout), grab with your hands and pull backward as you inhale. When your hands reach the starting position you can relax and take a single full breath before moving on to the next repetition.

6) Fist Clenching - This is a simple exercise to complete. Start with your hands fully open. Now begin to fully close and open your hands. You will want to do this as quickly

as possible. You should be able to at least complete 100 reps as quickly as possible.

7) Forearm Roller - You can either make a roller (as I have already described in iron forearms or buy one where they sell fitness supplies. To make on simply drill a hole in a thick wooden dowel (I'd use a dowel that is about 2.5' long) and tie a rope in the hole. Tie the rope to some weight. This setup is simple to use. Simple grip the roller and begin twisting it as though your are wringing out a wet towel. This will cause the rope to wrap around the dowel. Continue doing this until the weights reach the dowel. When the weights get heavy and you need more of a challenge. Stand on two chairs that are wider than shoulders distance apart and get into a half squatting position (Ma-Bo or horse stance). Place the roller on your thighs so the rope hangs between your legs and the chairs. now begin rolling up the rope and weights.

8.) Gripper Work - I also suggest you make regular use of spring hand grippers. The best can be found at any sporting goods store.. My late friend and mentor Joe Lewis (1944-2010) the first U.S. kick boxer and master of Okinawan karate) started using the strongest steel spring grippers in America and had amazing grip strength.

I like to set up my Dynamic Strengthening workouts in the following manner (a Thai kick boxing friend of mine gave me these suggestions):

1) Warm-up

2) Pushing and Pulling the Iron Block - 10 reps x 3 sets (30 seconds of rest between sets)

3) Alternate Fingertip and Knuckle pushups - Complete a set of knuckle pushups (rest 30 seconds) then complete a set of fingertip pushups. Repeat for 3-5 sets.

4) Dynamic Core Circuit:

5) Abdominal Wheel - 10-20 reps

6) Twisting - 10-20 reps

7) Side Bends - 10-20 reps (I sometimes use just one heavy dumbbell per side).

No rest between exercises, 30 seconds rest between circuits. Complete 3-5 circuits

8) Grippers - 3 sets of 5-10 reps with a heavy gripper

9) Forearm roller - 5-10 sets of rolling the weight all the way up.

10) 150 Fast Fist Clenches.

Impact Conditioning:

1) Self Slapping- To begin your iron body training you will start with regular palm slapping. This is a very simple ( and to onlookers very amusing). Start with a slap that is mildly uncomfortable. Over time you can work up to a harder and harder slap. Begin by slapping the entire surface of your torso (that you can reach). 5-10 rounds around your body should be enough. I also suggest slapping your forearms, thighs, and shins to condition them as well. You can also enlist the aid of a training partner. When using a partner stand in your typical fighting stance and have your partner slap predetermined areas of your body (front of the torso, thighs, back, ect...). When being struck make sure to focus your mind on the spot being struck. You should also tense the area as it is being struck. You should be proficient in this method before moving on.

2) Self Punching - The self punching method is identical to the slapping method except the fist are employed for striking as opposed to the palms. Remember to start with light strikes and over time begin hitting harder and harder. I recommend the use of a partner for this method as it is much more effective. You will have to know when to stop, so don't over do it. Always exhale just before you are struck in the abdominal region-never inhale

3) Medicine ball hits - You will need a partner for this method. You will also need to wear

an athletic cup. Simply stand in a high Horse stance (knees bent but not extremely so) with your guard up high to protect your face. Have your partner throw the medicine ball at your torso from all angles. Start light and over time work your way up to harder and harder throws. Bring your mind to the area being struck and tense to help you protect that area. You can also try lying on your back and have your partner drop the medicine ball on you. Start low and work your way up. When you get really advanced your partner can a bit of force to the drop.

Hands:

1) Paper Iron Hand - You will need to obtain an old, thick telephone book and some sort of stand to put the telephone book ( or stacks of old newspapers). The stand should be tall enough for the telephone book to be at your navel level. Make sure it is nice and sturdy. You will be striking the telephone book with the following hand surfaces:

a. Palms

b. back of the hands

c. knuckles

d. knife hand (shuto)

Some feel it is best to simple drop the hand onto the striking surface while others feel it is best to add some power to the strike. I feel the most effective way to develop the iron hand is to actually strike the target (as opposed to simply dropping your hand on the striking surface). As long as you take it easy in the beginning and slowly work your way up to striking the telephone book harder and harder you should never encounter any health problems or real injuries. Now you have to keep in mind that you will never be striking the telephone book as hard as you can. Even the Japanese Karate-ka, who are famous for their amazingly conditioned hands, never hit their makiwara as hard as they can. You should never need to hit the striking surface with more than half of you power.

For each surface of the hand you will need to complete 25-50 strikes or 100-300 strikes total per day.

I like to start with by conditioning my palms and the backs of my hands. I start with my right hand and strike with the heart of my palm, then immediately strike with the back of my right hand. I repeat this with the left hand and keep it up with a nice rhythm until I complete 25-50 reps. Then I shake out and stretch my hands before moving on to the next hand surface. Make sure to shake and stretch out your hands after each set of hand surface conditioning.

2) Heavy bag and focus mitt conditioning - When I work the heavy bag or focus mitts I wear a pair of leather gloves. When I'm done with my session I like to take the gloves off and work my strikes. I train the jab, the cross, rear hand palm strike, rear hand

knife-hand strike, lead backhand strike. I focus on single, hard strikes. I will usually do about 10-25 repetitions in this manner and my hand (especially my knuckles) are usually really red after this. I would recommend taking up this practice if you are serious about developing an iron hand.

After your training session you should do a full body stretch routine. I would also recommend obtaining a foam roller and use it to give yourself a self-massage or see a licenced professional massage parlor on a regular basis.

After your workouts you should shower if possible. Get the water as hot as is tolerable and let it wash all over your body (though, I'd avoid the face and genitals). Pay special attention to those areas you have conditioned that day and do not forget to run hot water over your hands. Before you get out lower the water temperature and let cold water wash all over your body. Again pay special attention to all striking surfaces including your hands. You can also opt to apply a good dit da jow liniment, especially on areas were there may be some bruising. If you are unable to find a good dit jit jow, you can also use witch-hazel. A witch-hazel rub can be found at any drug store. I find witch-hazel easier to come by and use it most often.

At first you should train your iron skills daily. Muscle conditioning exercises and Impact Conditioning will change from day to day. You should split your routine into "A" days and "B" days. On "A" days you will do your Ch'i kung, Static Core Work, and Impact Conditioning (hand conditioning). On "B" days you will do you Ch'i kung, Dynamic Strengthening exercise, and Impact Conditioning (body conditioning). Notice that Impact hand conditioning is done on "A" days when only static core work is done as opposed to "B" days where dynamic strengthening is done. All of the knuckle and fingertip pushups, and grip work on the dynamic strengthening day will weaken the musculature of the hand. You don't want to engage in impact hand conditioning when the musculature of your hands is weak. Damage to the tendons, ligaments, and bone structure would be much more likely. So, impact hand conditioning should be done with the static core strengthening exercises because those exercises stress the musculature of the hand to a lesser degree. Impact conditioning for the body is less strenuous on the tendons, ligaments, and bones so you don't have to worry about the dynamic strengthening exercises being detrimental to your impact training.

So in the beginning your week would look like this:

Monday: "A" Day

Ch'i kung (I do mine at 3 AM as this is the hour of th elungs).

Static Core Work

Impact Conditioning for the Hands

Tuesday: "B" Day

Ch'i kung

Dynamic Strengthening Exercises

Impact Conditioning for the Body

Wednesday: Same as Monday

Thursday: Same as Tuesday

Friday: Same as Monday

Saturday: Same as Tuesday (or rest).

Sunday: Rest (or start as Monday).

As you progress into more advanced stages you can incorporate your Ch'i kung and muscle strengthening exercises into a more traditional routine (I like to use the Static Core strengthening circuit as a finisher to some of my workouts). When you have developed your iron hand and iron body you will not have to condition them on a daily basis. If you do regular sparring and heavy bag work you should only have to do additional iron training once or twice a week.

The iron body student can absorb a strike by dissipation or by transferring this force via the bone structure to the ground. An advanced student will rebound this force from the ground, pass it threw his body, and back to the enemy. At more advanced levels of iron body, when an enemy strikes he is actually helping with your training, in fact the enemy may injure himself when he strikes you!

  Another technique in iron body training is "bone breathing" (not to be confused with the Japanese 'koppo' which is bone breaking at the weakest point with your strongest weapon or angle of attack). A student draws in external ch'i from the air to increase the strength of his bones. This is also called "washing the marrow". Tai Ch'i classics call this technique or result "iron wrapped in cotton". Even with your muscles relaxed, your bones feel as hard as iron.

# One finger jab

Originally I was pulling this chapter but I have a fondness for ancient legendary 'kungs' and rewrote this to make it more practical and interesting.

In the modern military certain groups learn to use the 'thumb' as a weapon to jab certain vital areas of the body. But in ancient China it was the middle or index finder that was developed as a weapon. In martial arts like Wing Chun Kung Fu, the forward jab is one (if not the fastest) offensive techniques to the eyes, or neck area.

The first part of this type of training will work provided you take time and let your finger and wrist adapt to the new striking method. The training after that which delves into the esoteric part of the kung. Could be legendary or the fact that no one is willing to spend the required amount of years training to do this amazing skill?

The first part of this 'one finger jab' training is just standing in an attack stance in front of a tree and jabbing either the same middle or index finder or alternating jabbing first the left and then the right middle or index finder. I would start with 100-300 strikes per finger everyday. After some time your skin could split (depending on how hard you are actually striking the tree). This will heal and continue training after a time you will note the skin where you have been striking will be much harder as well as the bone underneath and muscles. When you are able tio strike the tree at full power. You can begin the next phase of training striking a large boulder or brick wall. After doing this for five years. Begin striking a caste iron plate. When you can do this at full power. One strike to an enemy directed at his eye, temple, or neck could kill him instantly.

Now if you wanted to go on further still hang an iron bell or heavy block of iron or steel about five to six feet off the ground (the metal should weigh 15-20 pounds). Begin striking the metal with the same finger(s) as before and continue this everyday.

Now at some point (supposedly) you should start to notice that you can move the metal backwards without physically touching it! This is where the 'legend' may be come a tall tale or you become super-powered and able to merely point and kill someone. But no, it goes beyond this after you have reached the point of moving metal by the emission of ch'i threw your finger.

The next five years of training you merely point at a candle about ten paces away and put it out. Continue this everyday and every week move back three paces. Until you are able to put out the candle from a distance of over on hundred feet. Then place a glass cover around the burning candle and when you can put out the candle without breaking the glass you will have mastered the one finger jab!

# Training your reflexes

The need for superior reflexes is paramount to defeating your opponent. The younger you start training your nervous system the better you will be and more advanced fighting can be accomplished. When you train a repetitive action, over and over again, you develop a "reflex arc" that can almost act on its own, without conscious thought. Combined with strong intentional training on what or how your body will react given a certain stimulus is where we will begin your training. For example; when a punch is throw at your face or body. You will automatically either; block, dodge, or grab the arm of the enemy. You must practice this not only physically with your body but also mentally. While you sit or lie and relax, these exercises will be deeply embedded into your subconscious. Also a good mental exercise to do while you are waiting for the bus, on a subway, or walking, is to imagine the people around you attacking you in various ways. Imagine how you would react to the different types of attacks and the outcome. This exercise will keep you aware of all danger around you and train your mind to always be ready! Being always ready is another rule you should follow. Every morning before you leave your home, you should do your warm up exercises and be ready for action. Your home is where you dwell and should be your safe haven.

The one place you can (and need) to relax and be able to let your guard down. You need this home relaxation time just as much as you do training and exercise. This will help you remain sharp and strong. If you try to always be on guard it will wear you down and just like having chronic pain. It will begin to cause health and mental problems in your life. Make your home your sanctuary that is a safe clean environment to live, train, enjoy, and thrive in.

Begin upon awakening in the morning, before you even get out of bed stay on your back and stretch. Then rotate your wrists and ankles. Bend your neck from side to side gently and then sit up slowly and stand. Your body has been lying in bed dormant for overnight and needs to gently be warmed up so you do not injure yourself. This becomes more helpful as one grows older. You would be wise even if you are still under age thirty to warm up, always as small trauma will accumulate and cause various arthritis, joints, ligaments, and tendon problems when you do get older. Ancient to modern techniques have been used to train and activate your nervous system. This is a key element to your self defense component. "Hop scotch" was used by ancient Roman soldiers to develop reflexes and coordination. It is a game that can be done anywhere and is very effective. Skipping rope is another excellent method of getting coordination plus cardiovascular training. In fact skipping rope for only 15 minutes is equal to running for 30 minutes.

It can be done again anywhere and the equipment can be taken with you in your duffle bag or suitcase. Another good method is to get a solid rubber ball and push a length of line through the middle of it use a screwdriver and then tie a knot in the end that exits the bottom. You can then practice hitting the ball at various heights that you hang the ball from. The amount of time you spend doing this hitting, kicking, and even dodging the ball. Your eyes, and body will become accustomed to moving together and you will become more fluid in motion.

For your grip and hand strength, just obtain a good handful size piece of modeling clay from any art supply store(as I wrote about earlier). Take and roll it into a ball and then practice squeezing it over, and over again. You can do this while watching T.V. or reading swap hands and try to do at least 100-300 squeezes per day. Some basic warm up exercises should be done before every workout or in the morning before you leave your home.

1) Pull-ups 2) Side stretch 3) Twists 4) Shake your limbs 5) Proper breathing 6) Arm circles 7) Sit-ups 8) Leg raises 9) Push-ups 10) Squats

# Conditioning your body

You need to have a healthy strong body to come out on top. You do not have to be a huge muscular bodybuilder. But you do need to have a healthy body that you can rely on to defend yourself and save your life and those that you care about. Weight training will build up your strength and size the fastest. However, this may not be an option if you are traveling, or not able to get to a gym. If this is the case the following exercises will increase your strength, size, and stamina if followed on a regular basis. Try to include some of the following exercises at least every other day; push-ups, pull-ups, squats, sit-ups, crunches, and leg raises. Go to a gymnasium or consult an expert in physical development to aid you in obtaining and maintaining a strong healthy body.

You need to eat a healthy diet as well the following are the diet guidelines I recommend you follow these key points;

1) Eat slowly; it is not necessary to drink much while you are eating. Food should be thoroughly chewed so it is well combined with moderate amounts of saliva. Digestion starts in your mouth.

2) Try not to drink with your meals. Do not wash down your food.

3) Drink adequate amounts of water of water upon arising and between meals. Water

is the best liquid needed to purify your blood stream.

4) Eat to live. Do not live to eat.

5) You will find it helpful to eat at planned times. Permit from 2 to 3 hours to elapse between meals.

6) Do not eat before bedtime. Your stomach needs to rest along with the rest of your body.

7) It is best not to eat if you are emotionally upset, fatigued, or in pain. Either postpone or eliminate a meal if you are stressed.

8) Eat several small meals, rather than three large ones. The final meal should be light and several hours before you go to sleep. This also will allow you to still defend yourself. If you overeat your breathing will become labored and it will slow you down in defending yourself.

9) Avoid foods that are too hot or cold.

10) Increase your intake of raw fruits during breakfast. This will be a good source of enzymes that will aid digestion.

11) Eat more raw vegetables, especially salads, before your main course. This stimulates and aids digestion.

12) It is most healthy to seek variety in each meal, mix it up and enjoy your food.

Breathing and getting hit; are two of the most unused basic conditioning exercises that can be done anywhere and anytime.  Proper breathing will help increase the amount of oxygen in your blood stream and thus increase the amount of energy in your body.  Also, when you are being attacked exhale and contract your abdominal muscles. This will help minimize the damage to a strike here. If you inhale while throwing a punch or kick you will be off balance. Always exhale forcefully, perhaps include a yell to accompany your punch, kick, or throw as well.  Inhale while backing up or circling your enemy. Get in the habit of always going around your enemy and then attack. Do not let your enemy circle you!  Here is the breathing exercise you should practice all the time. This will also help develop your abdominal muscles to contract hard and can be done while sitting or standing at anytime.

Diaphragmatic breathing: Stand or sit with your mouth closed, inhale deeply through your nostrils. Keep your chest rigid and concentrate your thoughts on your diaphragm "tan tien" area. Let it expand as you count (in your minds eye) to eight. Hold your breath when you reach eight in your mental count, then slowly count to four. As you let go of your breath, on the mental count of four, compress your diaphragm down on your stomach muscles forcibly as you open your mouth to exhale. The first time you practice diaphragmatic breathing you may find yourself coughing especially if you are a smoker.

Do not be alarmed. You are simply not used to deep breathing. Repeat the exercise six times. You may find the sixth breath causes a slight dizziness. This is only confirms that you are unaccustomed to the absorption of this volume of oxygen. The oxygen that is absorbed quickly goes to your brain. You do not need to continue beyond six inhalations the first time you practice this exercise that increases your oxygen by 500% or more! This will over time give you a great advantage over an enemy that does not have well developed lungs and deep regular breathing is the way to achieve this most healthy of habits.

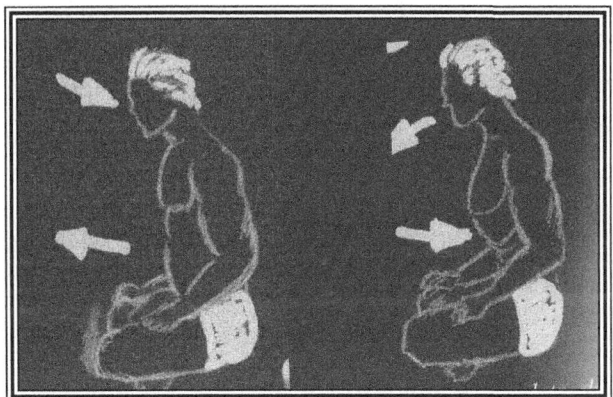

# Primary weapons

The human anatomy has plenty of weapons that can be in fact lethal. The advantage is that you are always armed with them and can never be disarmed. If you're natural weapons is all you use to defend yourself. Then you will not feel naked or at a loss. Like a person that relies on a firearm, or other external weapon. This gives you a huge psychological advantage verses a person that relies heavily on a gun, mace, tonfa, staff, knife, nunchuka, sai, or sword, the person that uses these weapons as the primary weapons, will always be reaching for them or have them close by. You will not have this disadvantage of never being without your weapon of choice with Demoncide-waza.

Here are your primary anatomical weapons that you always have with you.

1) Fingers; can be used to grab, stab, and jab. They are in your daggers.
2) Fist; can be used to pound, smash, and strike. This is your mace, short sword, and hammer.
3) Elbow; can be used to pound, smash, and strike. This is your pile driver, crowbar.
4) Knee; can be used to pound, smash and strike.
5) Forearm; can be used to block, and strike.
6) Foot; can be used to kick, block, and feint.

7) Head; can be used to smash with your forehead, and bite with your teeth.

The following six uses of your hands will first be addressed. They are the most used and the fastest weapon in unarmed combat that you can use to defend yourself. Great care must be taken when using these tools of destruction on another human being. You must also care that you flex your muscles and use these weapons once engaged with the enemy repeatedly, at the same time screaming or yelling at the enemy.

Get in the habit while training of throwing three successive strikes per arm, when you can do that for each of the six hand weapons, increase the number to six repeated thrusts per arm. This will greatly increase your fighting stamina and power when you do actually have to defend yourself.

Basic fist; is made by rolling your fingers back until your finger tips are pushing into your palm tightly and then fold over your thumb on the outside of your now closed fist. You will want to strike your enemy using the first to knuckles of your fist, or use the edge to smash down like a hammer, or even use a backhand.

~Basic fist~

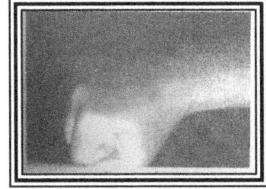

Edge of hand; is made by extending your fingers together and flat pressed against each other. This type of weapon is most effective against the neck, nose, and throat.

~Edge of hand~

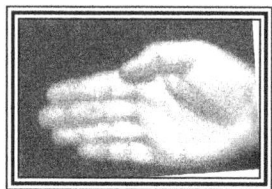

Thumb jab; this is just like the basic fist except you now extend the thumb outward while still pressed against your forefinger. Effectively used against the solar plexus, eyes, throat, and temples.

~Thumb jab~

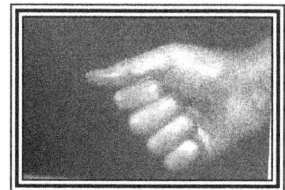

Cupped hands; is made like the edge of hand but cup your palms. Used to burst your enemy's ear drums if done correctly slapping both sides of the enemy's head at the same time, if done with enough force it will stun the enemy.

~Cupped hands~

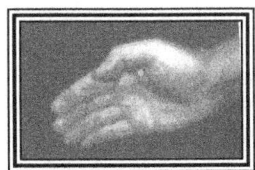

Finger jab; is made by pointing either one or two fingers that are held rigidly, most effective against the eyes or throat. This will inflict severe injury to the enemy.

~Finger jab~

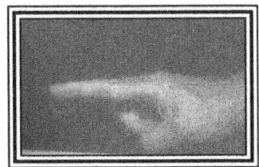

Heel of hand; is made by bending back slightly the open palm, but close your fingers down. You want to deliver a powerful strike using the heel of your hand. It can be used effectively against the jaw (as in an upper cut), directly to the face, head and solar plexus.

~Heel of hand~

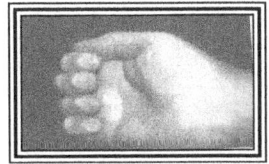

Remember when you are engaged in a fight for your life, the use of any object can also be used. You can make your enemy duck by throwing things, or even blind them by throwing dirt or sand in their eyes.

To make these weapons even more lethal, you can condition the striking points of each of them. This will also allow you to practice the strikes full force against the training box or bucket. Construct a wooden box about 25-30 inches square or obtain a standard five gallon bucket. Fill it with regular white rice just shy of six inches full. Stand or sit above it and practice all your hand strikes into the rice. This training will condition your striking points and joints, that will help reduce your natural sensitivity to impact. Take your time and continue this phase of the training for at least a month, then after a month of daily conditioning training. Empty the rice out and fill your training box or bucket with sand. This will further condition your striking points and cause calluses to develop on the striking area of your anatomical weapons.

Remember to inhale while pulling back your strike an exhale forcefully (even giving out a "ki-ai" shout or scream) and go as deep as you can into the sand try to hit the bottom. Do this for 10-15 minutes everyday as fast as you can. If you still think you need even harder striking points. Empty the sand and this time replace it with small gravel no bigger than the size of a pea. Make sure to massage your striking points and hands after every training session.

Another method of training is to take a stack of newspapers, tape them together along the outer edges making it at least six inches thick. You may then attach this against a brick wall or lay it down on top of a stack of cement blocks. Over time the newspaper will aid in the conditioning of your striking points. After a few months you will be able to strike the cement blocks without the newspapers there. This technique is used at various training centers throughout China. Like anything worthwhile it will take time to develop fully. However, these anatomical weapons are lethal even without the conditioning exercises. They will just make you even more lethal!

# Primary targets

Unlike other self-defensive methods, that uses non-lethal nerve centers for targets. The following are used only for life and death situations. It is the last resort when all else has failed.  You are utilizing your body's maximum strength against your enemy's weakest anatomical points. Which will result in death or disabling your enemy, attacking rather than defending is critical for you to be the victor instead of the victim! Always keep your balance and do not allow your enemy to grab any part of your body. Strike with the speed of a cobra and the power of a tiger. Strike and keep striking until you have disposed of the enemy.  If you do fall to the ground or are thrown with your enemy keeps continued strikes to your enemy. Remember you are in the fight for your life there is no second place here or "dirty fighting" anything goes.  During a fight you will not have time to stop and think about where to throw your strikes. That is why it is paramount that you practice, practice and practice! You can do this anywhere it is what boxers call shadow boxing. Imagine you're worst or most feared enemy and then proceed to throw your strikes at him while ducking and dodging your enemy's. Rehears in your mind what would you do if the enemy got you in a lock or hold?  You can practice kicks, grabs and throws and how you would get out of them. This is the basis for what is called "kata" in the martial arts. A kata is a sequence of learned moves and or combination of throws, kicks, strikes, ducking and dodging. That was once an actual fight from the distant past. This was a way in which legendary "moves" that work very well were preserved and past down through history, so that one did not have to re-discover them as the original martial arts master did. You can make up your own unique kata's of certain combination of "moves" you find are useful for you to defend yourself with, as everyone is of different size and shape. Martial arts styles also vary and are suited best to specific body types, for example; Choi le Fut Kung fu is almost unbeatable if the person learning it is above a certain height. Tall people and basketball players would be suited best with is style. Where, Shotokan karate is great for overall development. But the fact is, the more, well rounded muscular person who will excel at this style. A person shorter in stature would benefit from the Wing Chun Kung fu style and be very hard to beat. Then again it is the drive and person combination of physical and mental ability to win. A heavyweight boxer that uses only three punches (uppercut, jab and straight punch) will best a smaller black belt that has over one hundred moves at his disposal. If you do have the time to take martial arts, do so and learn everything possible. There is no substitute for actual physical contact and practice with a qualified martial arts instructor regardless of the style being taught. One myth that has kept coming up in training various groups of military and civilian personnel is that a upward strike to the nose will drive the cartilage into the brain and kill your enemy. Nothing could be father from the truth. The fact is the nasal cartilage cannot be driven through the skull into the brain. It is much softer than bone and a strike to the nose will only break the cartilage, cause temporary blindness (due to watering of the eyes) and some bleeding but absolutely not a lethal move. It will give you time to strike the eyes, throat and temples. Always assume your enemy is stronger and faster than you are. If they are armed with a firearm or knife, stand facing them with only one side of your body towards them.

Keep your distance do not engage them. If they do shoot you and you have no cover to shield yourself keep facing them and use your arm as a shield. If fired at you will have a better chance to live by allowing the bullet to first go through the arm rather than directly into your vital organs in your upper torso. The main thing to keep in mind is remain out of the line of fire. You do not have to be faster than a bullet, just move to the left or right out of the line of fire or where the gun barrel is pointed at. If you are within arms reach and you know you are going to be shot by your attacker as fast as you can move to one side and grab the gun and turn it bending your attackers wrist towards your enemy and if possible twist it out of their hand. If the attacker has a knife you might want to try kicking under his hand carrying the knife. But if possible stay away and keep your distance. Your enemy might be larger than you are. If so then when they attack grab whatever limb they attempt to strike you with first. For example; if they throw a punch grab and attack their arm. Or if it is a kick attack their leg. Then attack the "primary targets" you will learn in this chapter. The rule of thumb is always if your enemy is larger than you. Do not rush in to attack their "primary targets" If you do this before striking the enemy's secondary targets; i.e. elbow and knee joints you will be at a disadvantage and your enemy will have the reach advantage by virtue of the anatomical size difference. To cut your enemy down to size, you must first divide and then conquer. A 6'5" enemy might seem unbeatable. Until you attack the 2' ½" arm they throw at you. Break the joint, twist the hand, and yank in the fingers. Then with lightning speed attack the "primary targets" and you will defeat the enemy. The same applies to their leg is the attempt to kick you. Attack the knee joint by kicking at it from either side this alone has stopped many attackers before any harm comes to you or your loved ones. Remember most bullies and attackers do not expect you the victim to fight back with the fury of Black Dragon Kungfu! If possible retreat, re-evaluate, and then attack, but keep yourself alive at all costs! Always remember "A.B.C.; Always Be Cool" When someone is staring directly at you. Do not stare back. This will challenge the person looking at you and invite violent tendencies. Instead look up or stretch and yaw like you are bored. Some people are looking for a fight and just seek those out who they think they can beat up, in order to try to prove to themselves that they are better than you, because they suffer from low self-esteem and are really cowards. Remember 90% of self defense is just to avoid the trouble in the first place. You know what areas of the environment you live in will be trouble. Crowds always favor confrontations i.e. clubs, bars, concerts, major events, subway, elevators, trains, etc. Of you are walking and are brushed or bumped into by a fellow citizen, be the better person and even if it was not your fault, say "excuse me." Politely and move on. Do not start a shoving match or worse. These people coming in contact with you are innocent and Black Dragon Kungfu is to be used as a last resort always! Just as lethal as a firearm only it has an unlimited amount of ammo and can never be separated from you. Just knowing you have two fists full of potential kinetic dynamite, should give you an air of confidence that will keep away all but the hardcore thugs. People will notice this and then you can be more relaxed and make new friends instead of an enemy. To be admired and loved is always better than to be feared and loathed. Offer people your open hand of the protector, instead of a closed fist of the ever turbulent warrior. Peace should always be your goal in both your private and public life.

# Front targets

1) Temples; striking one or both of these vulnerable parts of your enemy will knock out or kill them!

2) Eyes; striking, gouging out the eyes, will stop the enemy. When this is done immediately strike the throat, which will double over the enemy and then deliver the kill strike to the back of the neck.

3) Throat; this is a multi target area, where the windpipe (trachea) can be smashed or stabbed. The neck can be broken, or either side of the neck struck with the edge of the hand.

4) Solar plexus; this large nerve center will disable the largest enemy. Strike in an upwards direction for maximum effectiveness. Straight line strikes can be deflected, always strike in an upward motion.

5) Groin; this area in both males and females if struck will cause instant pain. If kicked with sufficient force you may rupture the testicles.

Figure 13

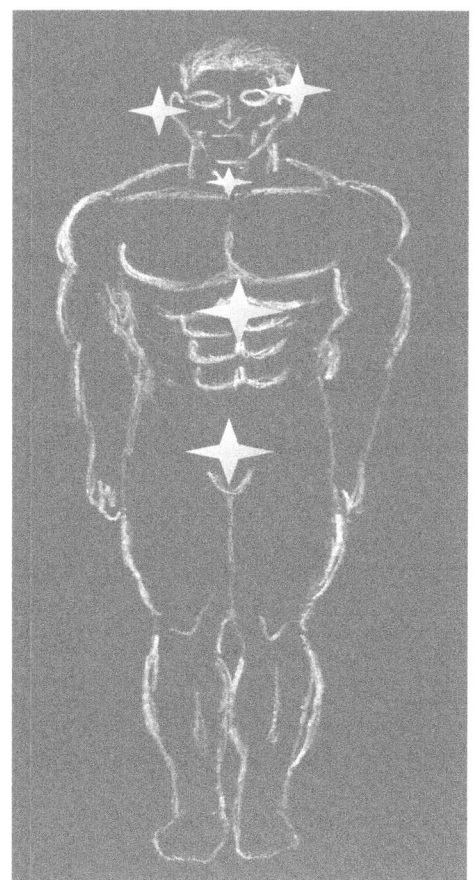

**Figure 13**

Black Dragon Kung Fu is literally very powerful death techniques. It is a composite system to be used only in life and death situations. This system may save your life or those you love and care about. It is not for play or to be practiced on anyone! The techniques are lethal and at the very least will cause the need for immediate medical attention to the person(s) that have had the unfortunate attempt to victimize you. If you use and apply what you have learned in this book you will walk with a new sense of confidence and power that others will notice around you. This air of supreme confidant power will be noticed by your friends and family and in fact your attackers will avoid you now and not seek you out.

# Back targets

1) Temples; these may be struck from either side.

2) Ears; while not a lethal strike. Simple "cupped hands or palms" if struck in a clapping motion with great force will bust the enemy's eardrums. Another technique not so well know is the often called the "Mr. Potato head." Grabbing one or both ears and yanking on them hard can result in ripping off the ear(s) and does not require a large amount of strength, this often stops an attack.

3) Neck; striking here can result at a minimum pain, unconsciousness or death. Depending on the amount of force generated during the attack.

4) Spine; anywhere along the spine may result in nerve damage and possible paralysis. The boney part above the middle of the shoulder blades is very effective.

5) Kidneys; direct striking to the kidney will result in blood loss and possible permanent damage that may result in death from internal bleeding.

Figure 14

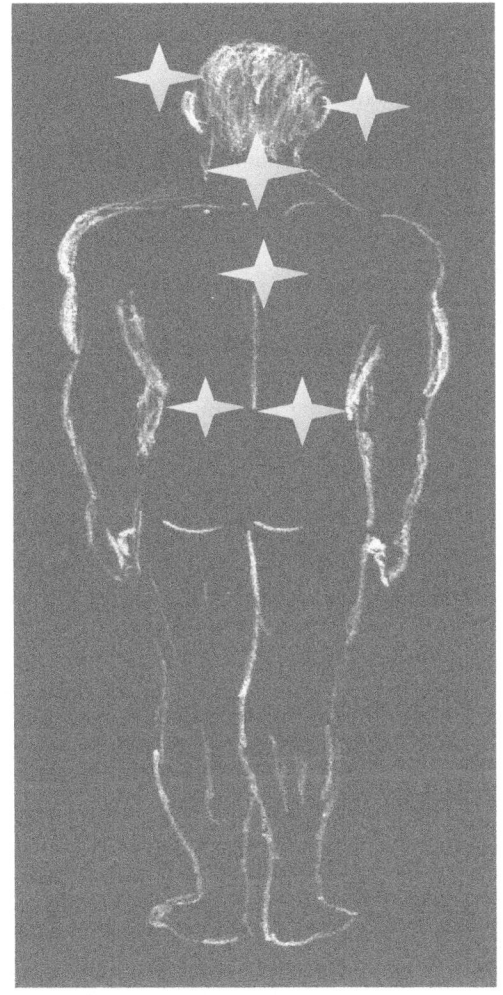

**Figure 14**

The reason for the low amount of targets is that you do not have to commit to memory hundreds of other vital striking points that may only cause the enemy pain. The ones listed do have the most lethal and immediate effect on any enemy so you can survive your hand to hand combat experience should the need arise.

When you are surprised or being attacked the most common reflex attack people do is usually hit the other in the face or jaw. This is not a good idea the nerves are clustered in the face and even a slap across the face will excite these nerves resulting in a more aggressive enemy. This is the last thing you want to have is a more enraged opponent. The adrenal glands will produce more adrenaline giving your enemy greater strength and speed. Your goal should be to knock out or kill your enemy as fast as possible. A life and death combat should not last longer than 30-45 seconds maximum! You want the attacker to stop as soon as possible so that you can either escape, or defeat him, by knockout or death.

The more intense the fight the shorter it will be. The less intense the longer it will last. The longer a fight goes on the greater chance you have to be injured or killed. You must use everything at you disposal that may include head butting use the forehead and torque to either the left or right side upon impact. You want to direct all your energy using the head butting technique or "nutting" as they call it in the United Kingdom. At your attackers nose or there eyes for maximum effectiveness. This may come in handy if you are caught in a bear hug by a larger enemy. If you are caught this way from the rear arch your back at the same time you smash the back of your head into your attackers face.

## Common objects as weapons

Besides your natural anatomical weapons, if you are attacked. Some common everyday objects may be utilized as offensive or defensive weapons. Some of these are; pen/pencil, walking stick or cane, the chair you are sitting on, the keys in your hand, the cup of coffee you are carrying, some coins you may have in your pocket, a rolled up newspaper, books you may be carrying, even rocks on the ground around you.  These can be your secondary weapons, as they are next in line of speed in availability. The reason why most weapons that are carried for the specific purpose of protection are not used is the element of surprise! The criminal has the distinct advantage of a laid out and planned attack on you, in order to assault, mug, rape or murder you! Even a professional bodyguard, military personnel, or law official, must let their guard down. Because the fact of the matter is they cannot be using their weapons that they are carrying on every person that  happens to just walk by them or merely look suspicious.  It gives the criminal or terrorist an advantage that they fully are aware of and exploit it all the time.

That is why you must mentally visualize and attack people as you stay "on- guard" for the real thing. It is no wonder so many of the armed forces are getting post traumatic stress disorder (P.T.S.D.) if you are young being exposed to this constant state of vigilant stress of war, will eventually leave its ugly mark on the strongest and bravest of military personnel. This is another reason why Black Dragon Kung Fu is so effective. Plain and simply it is always with you and will keep protecting you for life.

"Sparing is to what a sharpening stone is to a Samurai sword. It will keep your reflexes sharp and you on the edge ready to strike" Sifu-Tony Salvitti

# The law and defending yourself

This is perhaps one of the most important chapters of information that you need to know. It could very well save you from financial or criminal disaster. In the preceding chapters you have learned how to defend yourself and love ones. But the after effects are far reaching even though you are the innocent good law abiding citizen that was attacked. The legal system in the United States of America has been bogged down with so many legal cross references and amendments. That it is now open to anyone's interpretation and in the court of law it is only what you can 'prove' that the court will believe is a fact. This is regardless of zero to one hundred witnesses present at the 'alleged' crime. If you are a victim of an attack and a police officer shows up and begins speaking to you. Do yourself a favor and do not speak to them! The words "everything you say and do will be held against you." Are exactly that, remain silent and do not say anything until your attorney is provided for you or you use your own legal council. To the police officer you are nothing but a report he must do, and would rather not be involved in a court case that could last months. If your attacker is still alive this is very important. You could become liable for all the medical bills that the 'alleged' attacker now has because you were defending your life.

This has happened to me as well as a number of my friends in recent years. Plus a few even ended up going to jail themselves for "using excessive force" to defend their loved ones! The only mistakes they made were giving a statement to the police officer, at the crime scene while still hyped up on all the excitement and adrenaline flowing through their veins. Then to make matters worse taking the witness stand later on in there own defense because the 'alleged' attacker had a much better legal council to defend him. The information (if you do speak) will not be accurate and everything you say will be used out of context anyway. Indeed since you are victorious in your self defense, the police officer may see you as the aggressor! Since the release of all the adrenaline in your system will take at least 1-2 hours to metabolize and you will then be in a clam state of both body and mind.   This applies even more so to you 'if' you have defended yourself and actually killed your attacker. Do not speak or give any statement to any law official until after you have legal council.   No matter how intelligent you 'think' you are and your attacker is diseased lying on the ground. The state or country in which this crime and defense has taken place will represent your attacker in the court.  The only place that you will have the legal right to kill the attacker is if they are on or inside your property or residence. This still does not preclude you from speaking to the law official. Again keep silent and inform the law that you need your legal council provided as soon as possible. That is all you need to say. Do not resist the law officials or use any vulgar language or physical actions that could be interpreted as violent.  Indeed, cooperate with them in every other way and be nice and non-threatening to them. Just do not speak or give any written statement!  After you are provided with your legal council, explain everything to them in a calm manner. Do not leave anything out about the attack. Your legal council is on your side. If everything checks out you will be released and there should be no further problems.  However, if the 'facts' according to the investigation or the now deceased or attacker that lived and is now in the hospital, you could find yourself in the courtroom but only now your legal council must defend you.

You could be sued for thousands of dollars in medical bills, the attackers lost wages for not being able to go to work, mental stress (PTSD), and a host of other things that the 'attackers' legal council could find you responsible for and virtually ruin your life financially, and take valuable time from you and your family by having to be dragged through the court system that is now a joke.

This is why self defense begins by avoiding all confrontation before it escalates to violence. When you find yourself in a heated argument take a step back and a few deep breaths. This simple action could save you hundred to thousands of dollars. Even a simple shoving match can make you end up in a 'anger management' class that you will have to pay for and the court enforced 'anger management' will only make you really angry when you find out that you have to take time (that you do not have) and spend money you cannot afford to learn absolutely nothing! It is this author who has over 36 years in the martial arts and an excellent heavyweight fighter. To give you the advice of; simply walk away, leave; remove yourself from any violent situation. Yes, it is very sad case of irony to have spent decades learning arts in various martial arts and military hand to hand combat techniques, obtaining several black belts along the way as well as being a Master in both Tai Ch'i Chuan & Hsing-i chuan Kung Fu and not being able to use it. Because of the legal system I would instead duck or dodge out of the attack, let them hit me, or run away! You have now been armed with the knowledge to defend yourself with Kung Fu and the wisdom to avoid an attack in the first place.

I wish you peace in all your travels and long life.

Sifu-Tony Salvitti

Black dragon dojo

# Dit da jow formula

Dit da jow can be bought online and through martial arts catalogs or it can be directly obtained from a Chinese apothecary or master. Dit da jow is primarily used by martial artists to aid the healing of Iron Palm training. In addition natural oils such as olive oil, or peanut oil are excellent for massage both the top of your hands and palm and fingers. This will allow healing and recuperation from training your hands (or any other body part) faster because you help massage out the muscles and lymphatic system.

If you purchase Dit da jow already made, it is best that you purchase it bottled in glass and not plastic. Authentic Dit da jow that contains herbs like camphor, frankincense and myrrh, combined with alcohol can leach the chemicals from the plastic bottle and contaminate the liniment, making it totally useless or dangerous.

When you purchase the herbs to make your own Dit da jow, is in a glass jar or fired clay (porcelain or ceramic), and an alcohol medium like vodka or gin is used. Centuries ago Dit da jow was made by combining the herbs in a clay vessel and adding rice wine, then burying the vessel in the ground for months or even years; the longer the herbs sat in the alcohol, the stronger the Dit da jow became.

Many recipes are available; the ingredients listed here are merely examples. The best mixture depends on many factors, including the particular intended use. In particular, there are "toxic" and "non-toxic" recipes—the former must not be used on open wounds or ingested.

The herbs and other ingredients are typically coarse-ground, then steeped in alcohol (vodka or rice wine is commonly suggested), sometimes with heat, and then aged. Many vendors offer "herb packs" from which Dit da jow can be prepared, or pre-made Dit da jow mixtures for particular uses.

Traditional Chinese recipes vary greatly; some of the many possible ingredients are:

> Ba Ji Tian (Morinda root)
>
> Bai Bu (Stemona)
>
> Bai Dou Kou (White Cardamon)
>
> Bai Hua She (Pit Viper)
>
> Bai Ji Zi (Mustard Seed)
>
> Bai Shao (White Peony)
>
> Bai Zhi (White Angelica)

Ban Xia (Pinellia)

Cang Zhu (Black Atractylodes)

Cao Wu (Aconitum kusnezoffii or Kusnezoff Monkshood or Wild Aconite, a member of the large Aconitum genus)

Che Qian Zi (Plantain Seed)

Chen Pi (Aged Citrus Peel)

Chen Xiang (Aquilaria Wood)

Chi Shao (Red Peony)

Chuan Po Shi (Cudrania, in the genus Maclura)

Chuan Shan Long (Japanese Yam)

Chuan Wu (Sichuan Aconite)

Chuan Xiong (Ligusticum Root)

Da Huang (Rhubarb)

Dan Shen (Salvia)

Dang Gui (Angelica Root)

Dang Gui Wei (Angelica Root Tail)

Di Gu Pi (Lycium Bark)

Ding Xiang (Clove Bud)

Du Huo (Angelica Pub)

Du Zhong (Eucommia Bark)

E Zhu (Zedoary)

Fang Feng (Siler[disambiguation needed] Root)

Fu Hai Shi (Pumice)

Fu Ling (Poria[disambiguation needed])

Fu Pen Zi (Raspberry Fruit)

Fu Zi (Aconite)

Gan Cao (Glycyrrhiza uralensis or Chinese Licorice Root)

Gan Jiang (Ginger Root)

Gao Liang Jiang (Galangal Rhizome)

Ge Gen (Kudzu Root)

Gou Qi Zi (Lycium Berry)

Gu Sui Bu (Drynaria)

Gua Lou Ren (Trichosanthes Seed)

Gui Zhi (Cinnamon)

Hai Feng Teng (Kadsura Stem)

Hong Hua (Carthamus/Safflower)

Hua Jiao (Prickly Ash Pepper or Sichuan pepper(?))

Huang Bai (Phellodendron)

Huang Qin (Skullcap)

Ji Xue Teng (Millettia)

Jiang Huang (Turmeric)

Jiang Xiang (Dalbergia Rosewood)

Jie Geng (Platycodon)

Jing Jie (Schizonepeta)

Kuan Jin Teng (Tinospora cordifolia Stem)

Li Lu (Veratrum)

Liu Huang (Sulfur)

Liu Ji Nu (Artemisia)

Long Gu (Dragon Bone)

Lu Lu Tong (Liquidambar Fruit)

Luo Shi Teng (Star Jasmine Vine)

Ma Huang (Ephedra) or Gui Zhi (Cinnamon)

Menthol

Mo Yao (Myrrh)

Mu Dan Pi (Mountain Peony)

Mu Gua (Quince Fruit)

Mu Tong (Akebia)

Mu Xiang (Aucklandia lappa or Saussaurea)

Niu Xi (Achyranthes)

Pu Gong Ying (Dandelion)

Pu Huang (Cattail Pollen)

Qian Nian Jian (Homalomena)

Qiang Huo (Notopterygium incisum)

Qin Jian (Gentian Root)

Qing Pi (Citrus Peel)

Rou Cong Rong (Cistanche)

Rou Gui (Cinnamon Bark)

Ru Xiang (Frankincense)

San Leng (Sparganium or Bur-Reed)

San Qi (Panax pseudoginseng)

Shan Zhu Yu (Cornus Berry)

She Chuang Zi (Cnidium Seed)

Sheng Di Huang (Rehmannia)

Shu Di Huang (Cooked Rehmannia Root)

Song Jie (Pine Branch)

Su Mu (Caesalpinia sappan or Sappan Wood)

Tao Ren (Peach Kernel)

Tian Ma (Gastrodia)

Tian Nan Xing (Arisaema)

Tu Bie Chong (Eupolyphaga or Eupolyphaga sinensis Walker or Wingless Cockroach)

Tu Si Zi (Cuscuta Seed)

Wei Ling Xian (Clematis Root)

Wu Jia Pi (Acanthopanax)

Wu Ling Zhi (Squirrel Droppings)

Wu Wei Zi (Evodia Fruit)

Xi Xing (Wild Ginger)

Xiang Fu (Cyperus nut)

Xu Duan (Dipsacus Root)

Xue Jie (Dragon's blood)

Yan Hu Suo (Corydalis)

Yu Jin (Turmeric Tuber)

Ze Lan (Bugleweed)

Zhang Nao (Camphor)

Zhi Ke (Bitter Orange Peel)

Zi Ran Tong (Pyrite)

Zi Su Ye (Perilla Leaf)

Zi Wan (Aster Root)

Westernized recipe ;

Some recipes instead use ingredients more readily available in the West. These are obviously non-traditional, and some practitioners of traditional Chinese medicine would not consider such recipes "true" Dit da jow. A Westernized recipe might include ingredients such as:

Arnica Blossoms (anti inflammatory)

Blessed Thistle (blood purifier)

Cinnamon bark

Comfrey (anti inflammatory)

Ginger Root (circulation/wound healing)

Goldenseal Root (antibiotic)

Myrrh (antiseptic/wound healing)

Pseudoginseng (blood dispersion)

Rhubarb root

Sarsaparilla Root (blood purifier)

Witch Hazel (anti inflammatory)

~~~~~~~~~~~~~~~~~~~~~~~~~~~~~~~~~~~~~~~~~~~~~~~~~~~~~~~~~~~~~~~

Any combination of these healing herb's may be used. Over the centuries many combination's have been exploited (some better than other's). However, the one key ingredient has been a type of fermented alcohol. This can be vodka, wine, etc.

Some applications that should be noted is; never drink the homemade liniment use only on the hard trained external parts of the body. This is namely the palms of the hands, joints and fingers, knuckles (from consistent striking), toes, and feet 9outside edge of the foot and heels).

# Black Dragon Dim Mak

## Part II

# Copyright 2017
# Tony Salvitti

## ~WARNING~

The techniques, training methods, and application in this book are for informational purposes only. Serious injury and death can result in preforming or training with any of them.

The purpose is to provide rich centuries old historic and factual training methods. That may have been lost in time and not handed down from master to disciple. In regards to the reality of developing some of these fascinating abilities. The very fact that one has to dedicate many years to this study, insures that the disciple will master it and during the long years of training master themselves as well.

~Contents~

Introduction—112

Rules of Dim Mak—114

Weather & timing—117

Dim Mak Chart one—132

Dim Mak Chart two—133

Basic biology & anatomy—135

Weapons of the hand—145

How to kill a king—159

Cinnabar Palm—170

The lying tiger— 173

Clamping and locking fingers— 175

More Ancient "Kungs"—177

Ancient Chinese Dim Mak— 183

Glossary— 200

## Introduction

Revealed in this book for the first time is one of the most treasured secret and forbidden techniques ever devised in Black Dragon Kung Fu.

These techniques of "Dim Mak" also called the 'touch of death', the practitioner is advised to be extremely careful in its application. Once you have trained diligently for years-you cannot undo this new found powerful skill.

In the ancient days of India and China, 'Dim Mak" was used only when monks, Lamas, or royalty was endangered. Under these circumstances it was a matter of kill or be killed.

The practice of this lethal and advanced dark, internal Black Dragon Kung Fu Dim Mak, can only be mastered by long hours, which will culminate into years of patience, study, perseverance, self discipline , **and hard training.**

## 本書介紹：

本書首次提及國術中一種披染用而珍如的招式。在練習這种屬於點脈功夫—又名「致命棍之時」，習武者必被鄭重警告：出手時定須對手萬分小心。

從前，使用這種武術的人，通常但是活在暴政下為著保衛自己及家人的農民與僧人。在這般情形下，絕向實不容行何「公平比武」；而結果往往是「殺或被殺」。

對這門武術充滿希望的習武者須緊記—若想達到出神入化的境界，便不能不長期地持著恆心，努力鑽研和勤加苦練。

## Rules of Dim Mak

In the ultimate successful application of Dim Mak. The following points must be taken into consideration.

1) The correct bodily weapon to use.
2) The direction of the strike.
3) Proper breathing control.
4) The age of the target (mark).
5) Sex of the target (mark).
6) The degree of each strike.
7) The number of strikes needed.
8) The touching technique.
9) The muscular structure of the target.
10) The weather and time.
11) The action time before application.
12) The coordination ability of the target.

This book is written for protection of life and once this path is launched, the course cannot be undone.

Certain ch'i channel's (meridians) will be set up in your finger's and hands. They are in effect set to kill! Caution must then and in the future be used when holding everything from a flower to a baby, or your love.

The wrong grip, hold, or touch could result in the death or one becoming gravely ill.

## 點脈的敉大綱要：

練點脈的基本成功要素，有如以下數點：
(一) 正確地利用身體各部份作兵器。
(二) 出招的方向。
(三) 良好調氣法。
(四) 對手的年齡。
(五) 性別。
(六) 出招氣力的輕重。
(七) 不多不少的出手次數。
(八) 招無虛發。
(九) 對手的體格。
(十) 天氣與時間。
(十一) 交手用的運動。
(十二) 不相上下的對手。

Weather

As the influence of weather temperature is also critical to this technique. The weather is classified as follows;

1) Warm...............Between 75 to 90 degree F.

2) Hot....................Above 90 degree F.

3) Cool..................Between 60 to 75 degree F.

4) Cold.................Below 60 degree F.

## Daily hours timetable for Dim Mak

Certain vital point of the human body are more vulnerable to attack at certain hours of the day. Some are also stronger at certain hours of the day.

Should any one of the vital points be struck within the sensitive period of time the injury caused will be more serious than other hours of the day/night.

In the charts that follow are the vulnerable points each designated with a number.

Please study and memorize all of the vital points and times at which they should be struck for maximum effectiveness.

Of course the vital points will work at anytime of the day or night. But the maximum effectiveness they should be struck during the correct time. The amount of force and ch'i (life force) needed to inflict the same amount of damage will of course vary due to the factors of time, weather and temperature.

天氣。
　既然天氣對這門武術極有影響，且將天氣分列如下：
(一) 暖 — 華氏七十度至九十度之間。
(二) 熱 — 超過華氏九十度。
(三) 涼 — 華氏六十度至七十五度之間。
(四) 冷 — 低於華氏六十度。

　點脈的日常時間表。
　在一日的某段時間當中，人體內的部份命脈，是比較脆弱的。假如某條脆弱部份的命脈於這段脆弱時間內被傷，傷勢一定比平時來得重。下圖指示出脆弱命脈和它們較易被傷的時間跟天氣。

Dim Mak weather and time table (warm)

1-------------------12 pm to 2 am

2-------------------1 am to 3 am

3-------------------6 pm to 8 pm

4-------------------2 pm to 6 pm

5-------------------6 pm to 10 pm

6-------------------2 am to 4 am

7-------------------2 am to 5 am

8-------------------8 pm to 9 pm

9-------------------4 pm to 6 pm

10------------------1 am to 3 am

11------------------2 pm to 6 pm

12------------------4 am to 7 am

13------------------3 am to 7 am

14------------------1 pm to 4 pm

15------------------10 pm to 2 am

16------------------7 am to 10 am

17------------------6 am to 7 am

18------------------9 pm to 12 pm

19------------------8 am to 9 am

20------------------12 pm to 2 am

21------------------3 pm to 3 pm

22------------------10 am to 1 pm

23------------------10 pm to 11 pm

24------------------3 am to 8 am

25------------------12 pm to 2 pm

Dim Mak Hot weather 90 degrees F times.

1)------------------12 pm to 3 am

2)------------------ 1 am to 4 pm

3)------------------8 am to 9 pm

4)------------------4 am to 7 pm

5)------------------4 pm to 6 pm

6)------------------9 pm to 11 pm

7)------------------3 am to 7 am

8)------------------1 pm to 4 pm

9)------------------11 am to 1 pm

10)------------------9 pm to 1 am

11)------------------3 am to 7 am

12)------------------11 am to 12 pm

13)------------------12 pm to 2 am

14)------------------7 am to 10 am

15)------------------11 am to 1 pm

16)------------------12 pm to 3 am

17)------------------9 pm to 12 pm

18)------------------1 pm to 4 pm

19)------------------8 pm to 9 pm

20)------------------6 pm to 9 pm

21)------------------1 pm to 4 pm

22)------------------5 pm to 6 pm

23)------------------7 am to 10 am

24)------------------8 pm to 9 pm

25)------------------7 am to 10 am

点穴气象和时间表

指示： 气候强烈胜过九十度F

(一) 中午十二点至中夜三点
(二) 中夜一点至下午四点
(三) 中午八点至夜间九点
(四) 中夜四点至夜间七点
(五) 下午四点至下午六点
(六) 夜间九点至夜间十一点
(七) 中夜三点至中午七点
(八) 下午一点至下午四点
(九) 中午十一点至下午一点
(十) 夜间九点至中夜一点
(十一) 中夜三点至中午七点
(十二) 中午十一点至中午十二点
(十三) 夜间十二点至中夜二点
(十四) 中午七点至中午十点
(十五) 中午十一点至下午一点

(十六) 夜间十二点至中夜三点
(十七) 夜间九点至夜间十二点
(十八) 下午一点至下午四点
(十九) 夜间八点至夜间九点
(二十) 下午六点至夜间九点
(二一) 下午一点至下午四点
(二二) 下午五点至下午六点
(二三) 中午七点至中午十点
(二四) 夜间八点至夜间九点
(二五) 中午七点至中午十点

Dim Mak Cool weather 60-75 degrees F

1)--------------------12 pm to 6 am

2)--------------------1 am to 6 am

3)--------------------6 pm to 9 am

4)--------------------1 pm to 3 pm

5)--------------------9 pm to 12 pm

6)--------------------9 pm to 11 pm

7)--------------------1 pm to 4 pm

8)--------------------1 pm to 3 pm

9)--------------------12 pm to 3 am

10)--------------------1 pm to 3 pm

11)--------------------9 pm to 11 pm

12)--------------------7 am to 10 am

13)--------------------12 pm to 3 am

14)--------------------8 am to 10 am

15)-------------------8 pm to 9 pm

16)-------------------3 am to 7 am

17)-------------------9 pm to 12 pm

18)-------------------1 pm to 4 pm

19)-------------------7 am to 10 am

20)-------------------7 am to 10 am

21)-------------------5 pm to 6 pm

22)-------------------11 am to 1 pm

23)-------------------1 pm to 4 pm

24)-------------------7 pm to 11 pm

25)-------------------3 am to 7 am

<u>点穴气象和时间表</u>：

指示： 凉气候六十度至七十五度F之间。

(一) 夜间十二点至夜间六点

(二) 中夜一点至午前六点

(三) 下午六点至中午九点

(四) 下午一点至下午三点

(五) 夜间九点至夜间十二点

(六) 夜间九点至夜间十一点

(七) 下午一点至下午四点

(八) 下午一点至下午三点

(九) 夜间十二点至中夜三点

(十) 下午一点至下午三点

(十一) 夜间九点至夜间十一点

(十二) 中午七点至中午十点

(十三) 夜间十二点至中夜三点

(十四) 中午八点至中午十点

(十五) 夜间八点至夜间九点
(十六) 中夜三点至中午七点
(十七) 夜间九点至夜间十二点
(十八) 下午一点至下午四点
(十九) 中午七点至中午十点
(二十) 中午七点至中午十点
(二一) 下午五点至下午六点
(二二) 中午十一点至下午一点
(二三) 下午一点至下午四点
(二四) 夜间七点至夜间十一点
(二五) 中夜三点至中午七点

Dim Mak Cold weather below 60 degrees F

1)--------------------12 pm to 8 am

2)--------------------12 pm to 8 am

3)--------------------1 pm to 4 pm

4)--------------------6 pm to 9 pm

5)--------------------1 pm to 3 pm

6)--------------------7 am to 10 am

7)--------------------1 pm to 3 pm

8)--------------------8 pm to 9 pm

9)--------------------4 pm to 6 pm

10)--------------------2 pm to 4 pm

11)--------------------8 pm to 9 pm

12)--------------------9 am to 1 am

13)--------------------3 am to 7 am

14)--------------------8 am to 10 pm

15)--------------------9 pm to 1 am

16)--------------------11 am to 1 pm

17)--------------------6 pm to 9 pm

18)--------------------7 am to 10 am

19)--------------------2 pm to 4 pm

20)--------------------5 pm to 6 pm

21)--------------------8 pm to 9 pm

22)--------------------8 am to 9 am

23)--------------------8 pm to 9 pm

24)--------------------11 pm to 12 pm

25)--------------------7 am to 10 am

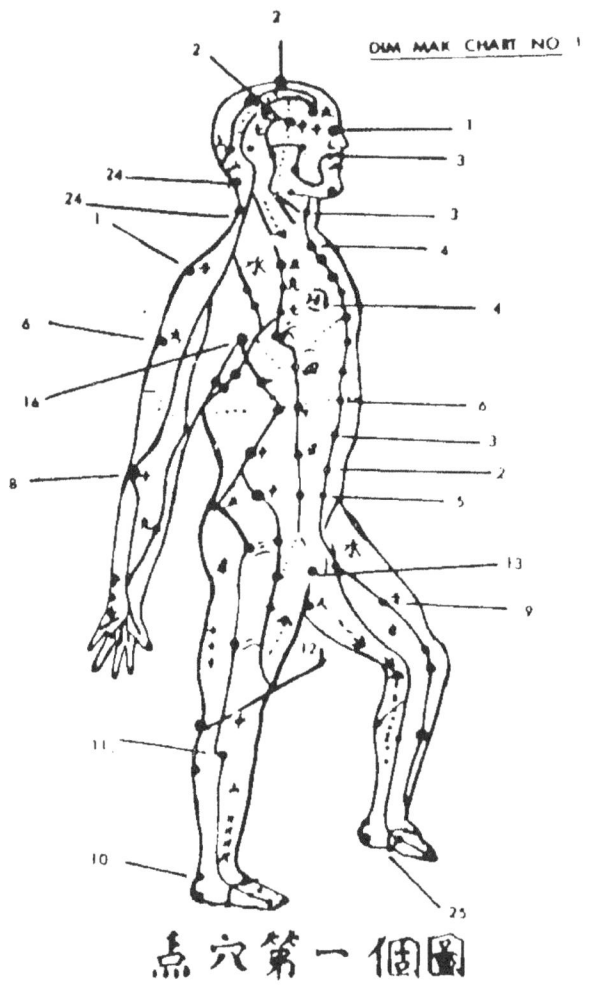

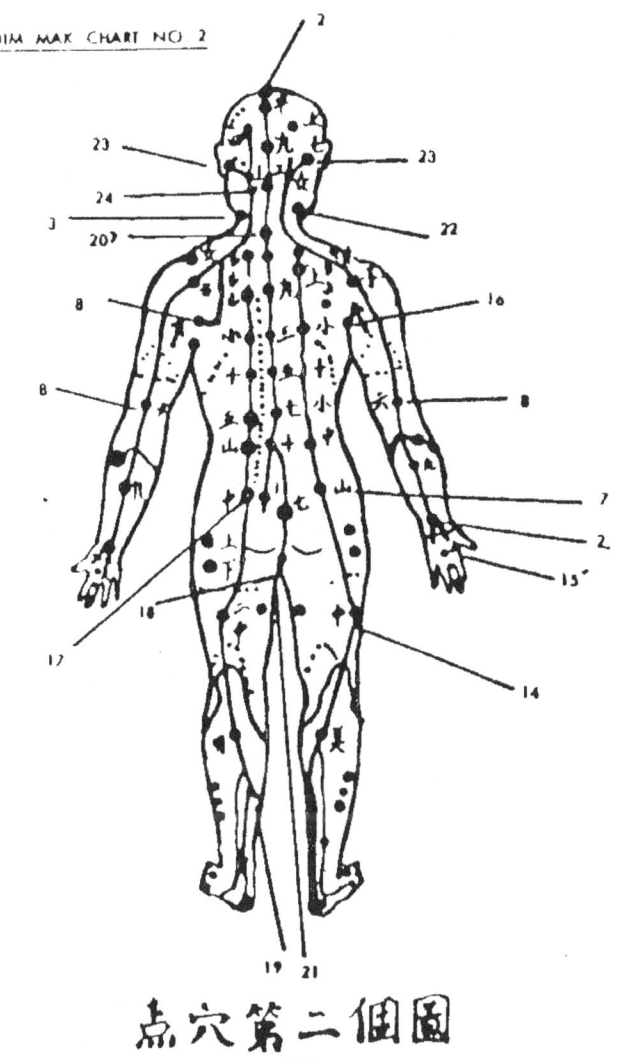

## Time table chart of the direction ch'i flows

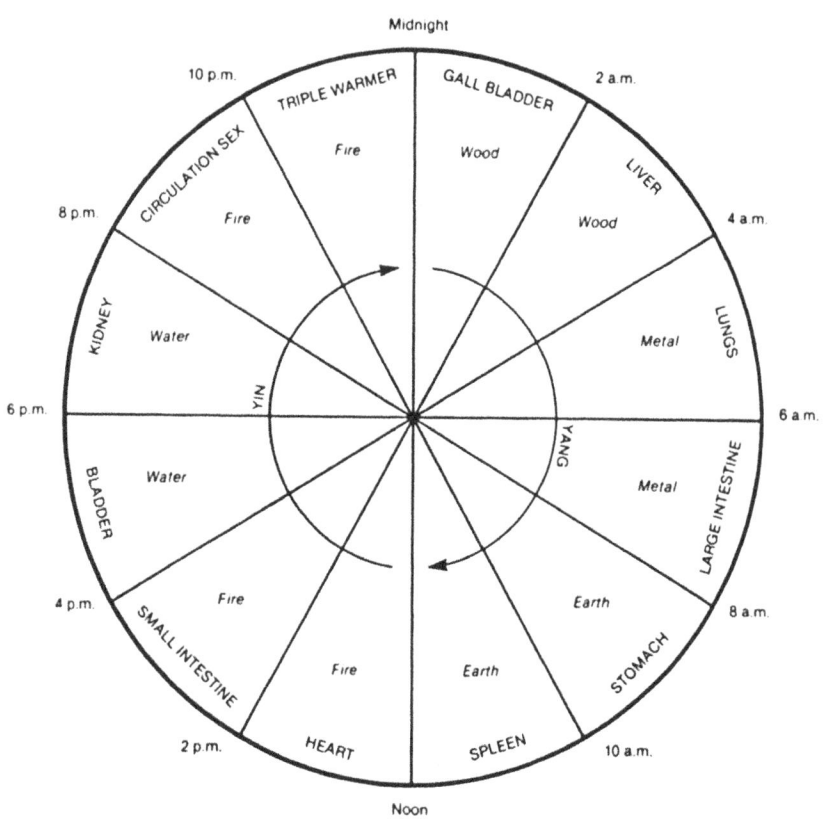

## Basic biology & anatomy

Any system that has existed for over 3,000 years, must have some factual properties to it. Dim Mak, is one of those areas that for some martial artist's borders on the paranormal. Some of the questions that will be answered here are;

1) Are the vital points of the body located and can a single strike result in death?

2) Are the vital points that can incapacitate a much larger enemy?

The answer to both of these questions is yes! But let us explore this in a bit more detail.

The central nervous system (CNS), which consists of the brain and spinal cord, serves as the control center of the human body. The normal brain function consists of billions of cells that are acting in a delicately balanced electrochemical series of events.

It is easy to disrupt this system with mechanical force. This leads to loss of consciousness or possible death.

This loss of consciousness or function can be brought on by several means, but two methods are the most common.

1) A direct strike to the head or surrounding structures with a transfer of accelerating-decelerating forces to the brain.

This causes the brain to strike the inside surface of the skull, leading to swelling of the brain tissue. If the force is severe enough it can actually cause shearing of the brain tissue, the result of which can be permanent injury and or death.

2) Temporary or permanent cessation of blood flow to the brain. This results in lack of oxygen, and immediate disruption of the brain.

Peripheral nervous system (PNS), controls the functions of the muscular system and can be attacked at various points all over the body. A strike or sustained pressure to a nerve can bring about significant disruption of the attackers body.

Another means of incapacitating an enemy is an attack directed at the cardiovascular system.

The methods here deals mainly with altering the hearts rate of pumping blood or the volume of blood being pumped. The rate at which the heart beats is determined by a number of factors. It has its own inherent rate determined by a number of factors.

This rate is determined by the sinus node in the upper chambers of the heart. This node sets up the hearts basic rhythm; however, this rate can be influenced by a number of factors.

One of the most important is nerve control.

The vagus nerve exerts an effect upon the heart to slow down the rate at which it beats. If the rate is slowed down, blood flow to the brain will result in one being knocked out. A strike to the carotid sinus nerve in the neck at the angle of the jaw will result in rapid slowing of the heart beat and drop in blood pressure.

Even a direct strike to the chest, if enough force is applied will result in electrical or mechanical failure of the heart-result death.

Anything that decreases the amount of returning blood to the heart through the venous system may result in a drop in blood pressure.

There are several factors that come into play here, but a severe strike to the body resulting in enough pain may result in blood pooling up in the venous system or surrounding tissues. Thus, the enemy will faint.

In this regards the internal organs of the abdomen are vulnerable to an injury of this nature as they have no skeletal structure for protection. A rupture of any or all of the liver, spleen, kidneys, stomach, pancreas, bowel, or bladder. Can lead to internal bleeding either slow or fast. Resulting in shock, or a slow delayed death.

A strike could result in a partial tear of the capsule of the organ with formation of a blood clot at the point of injury. This injury is still at risk for further bleeding and often results in the so-called "delayed death" due to massive slow internal bleeding.

A rupture of the intestine due to direct strike to the abdomen, although unlikely, can result in the generalized infection of the abdominal cavity called "peritonitis". The result is a slow painful death. Unless medical intervention is preformed on the "mark" within hours to days he will not live and mission complete status will be the result.

This is very effective against "marks" that have the fear or dislike going to seek physicians or medical treatment and can stand large amounts of pain. They hesitate as long as possible until the pain is too severe and end up passing away in bed or falling face first on the floor.

In any case you will be long gone with days set between you and the "mark" and as long as you set the ususal barriers of connecting you to the area where the "mark" was or contact with the. You will get away home free.

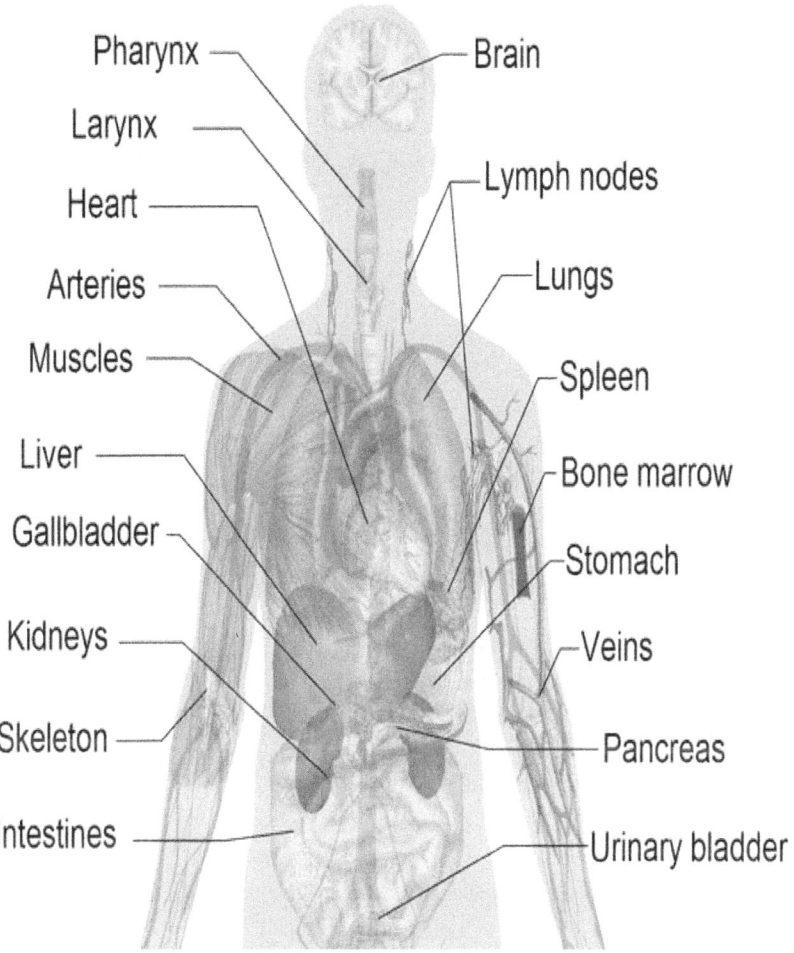

The most vulnerable portion of the respiratory system is the trachea (windpipe), or the larynx voice box). It is exposed in the front of the neck making it extremely easy to injure and seriously damage. A strike here can cause immediate swelling and death due strangulation as the swelling closes off the trachea. A minimum amount of force or pressure is all that is needed to fracture this part of the anatomy.

Fracture of the ribs can result in the puncture of a lung. This results in a collapse of the lung and loss of function.

Dim Mak, is the art of death striking. In Japanese martial arts this is called "Atemi" or "Yubi waza"- striking nerve center's. In addition the Japanese "Koppo" was used to inflect various bone breaking upon an enemy sometimes to immobilize the enemy without killing them.

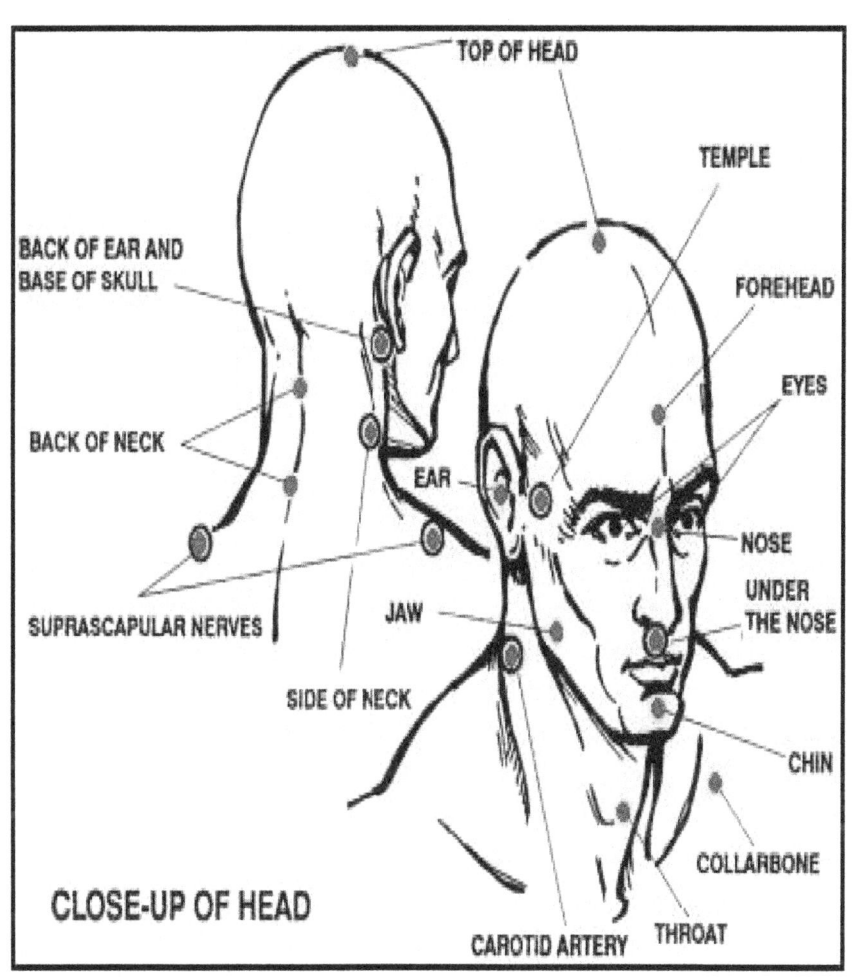

The two areas of the human body that you 'should not strike' are;

1) The top of the human skull.

2) The pelvis.

The reason is the top part of the skull is the hardest part. Also the pelvis 'hip bone' may result in you injuring your hand.

As I stated before the 'top of the head' is to be avoided. Some other vital points are shown here as well. A ridge hand strike directed against the 'temple' or 'back of neck' could result in instant death. Cupped hands against the ears will burst the ear drums, and finger strikes are effective into the eyes of the enemy.

## Weapons of the hand

To be most effective you should condition the weapons of your hands that you will be using to strike with and kill your enemy.

The conditioning of your body will also benefit you in many ways. The adaptation is due to stress imposed upon the body or body parts. Stressors, that will cause your body to adapt are;

1) Exercise- Tai Ch'i Chaun, to Jujitsu, or heavy weight training and Calisthenics.

These all will increase your muscle strength and bone density!

2) Repeated striking- kicking, falling, jumping, running, tumbling, walking and striking. Your skeletal system, and tissues will change and become harder, and firmer

The way a Samurai sword is made harder than a regular sword. Is the repeated beating and folding of the steel. Over and over again. Sometime it is done for three days straight! This causes extra crystalline structures to form in the matrix of the steel. Filling gaps on a microscopic scale. The result is a much harder and denser steel sword.

The same principle applies to your skeletal system. Repeated striking of the bones over a period of time. Will cause micro-fractures in the affected bone.

Over time these heal and the bone becomes much harder and denser than before! More so than an average untrained person. An example of this would be karate practitioners first two knuckles. They are more pronounced, and harder than an average persons.

The following anatomical weapons of the hand may be trained and conditioned, in order to strike the vulnerable vital points and cause maximum damage to the enemy.

To condition the striking parts one must commit to training over several months at a minimum to be effective. First start striking uncooked rice in a bucket or contained in a bag 300-1,000 times per day

Then after a month or two switch to striking a bucket of sand or small pebbles. This is often more than enough conditioning to effectively kill an enemy with strikes to the vital points. However, if you want to still go harder and more density can be achieved by then striking caste iron or a bucket of iron shot.

The weapons

The hand is 'cupped' fingers and thumb held tightly together, and bending the fingers and thumb slightly making the palm cup.

Highly effective against the ears of the enemy when slapped simultaneously. This can rupture or burst the ear drums. Resulting in great pain, or temporarily stunning the enemy.

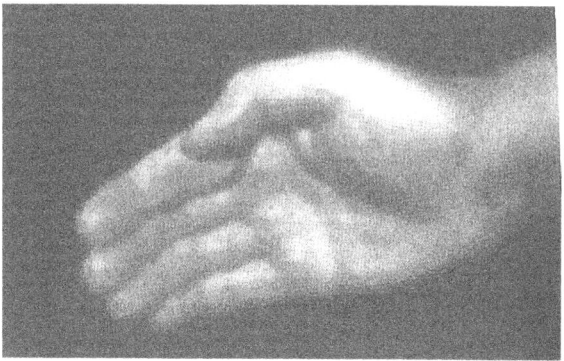

The fist is made by squeezing in and curling in the fingers making the knuckles of the hand very pronounced. These knuckles must be punched into the rice, then small pebbles and finally int steel shot.

Over time your knuckles will become more pronounced and very hard.

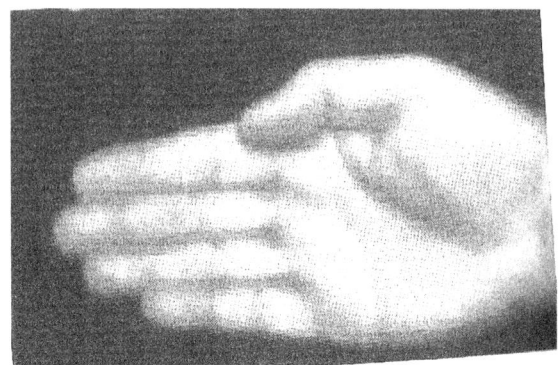

The edge of the hand. Bottom part below the little finger. This is very effective against the neck carotid arteries and vertebrae on the back of the neck. Also a sideways chop against the temple on either side fo the enemies head.

Start by striking a break or hardwood with newspapers, and gradually reduce the amount of paper until you are striking directly on the break or board.

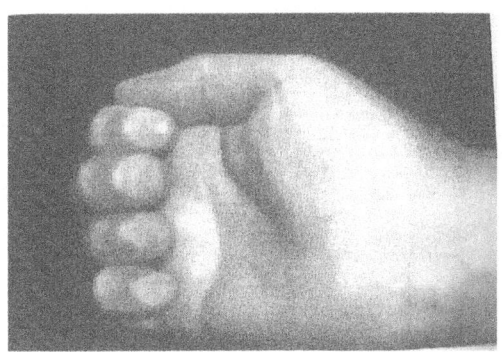

The 'heel' of the hand can be used with great force and applied against the chest, head, neck, or abdominal area.

Again it may be conditioned by first striking it repeatedly over and over against wood and eventually cast iron. The heel of the hand is already even without conditioning very strong.

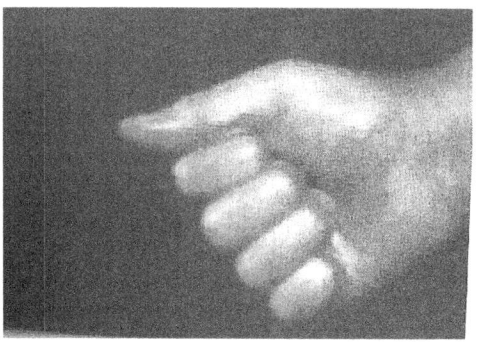

The thumb can be a very effective striking weapon. It is already one of the strongest digits you have. It is effective against the temple area of the skull, eyes, neck, groin and abdominal areas.

To condition start with a bucket of uncooked rice and strike into it 300-1,000 times per day. Later pour out the rice and start using small pebbles and continue until satisfied.

Obtain a strong metal or plastic bucket. A 5 gallon one is best and will allow you to practice going deep and if you start with rice for 3 months. Then proceed to small pebbles, for another 3 months. And continue on eventually adding iron ore or shot for another 3 months. Your hand weapons will now be very lethal and it will be impossible to disarm you.

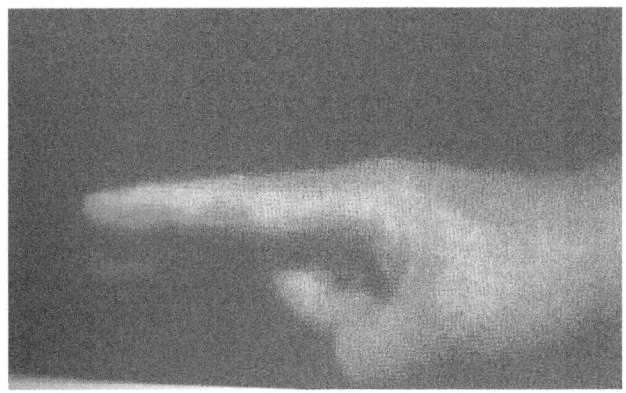

The index or middle finger (or both). Is an very fast and effective striking weapon against the eyes, neck, throat (larynx), and abdominal area.

Start conditioning the fingers a few months prior to using them. Start with a bucket of uncooked rice and after a month or two add small pebbles and eventually iron shot.

The end of your finger will now be in effect a iron poker.

In addition to your arsenal of hand weapons. You have your legs-the knee, brought up into the abdominal area, or grasping the back of the enemies neck and pull violently downward as your knee is thrust upward into the face, temple, or neck will result in a disabling strike.

Kicks- while high kicks (above the waist & jumping kicks) are dazzling to display. They are in fact not effective or fast enough to render your enemy defeated fats enough.
Indeed, a high kick may be intercepted and effectively blocked and counter-punched or worse with ease. The kicks you witness in fictional movies are not what is used to save your life.

Low kicks to the enemy's ankle, knee, and thigh, can be enough to immobilize him so you can get away and not have to cause any more harm. Remember your kicks are always slower than your hand strikes.

"A punch or kick should be felt and not seen!" ~Sifu Salvitti

Practice your speed as this combined with your physical mass of your arm, leg, or entire body will equal your total force. As in the following equation;

$$F = M \times A$$

Force equals mass times acceleration!

Your mass is the weight and is constant during battle. Your velocity/speed however is under your control. The higher the speed the proportional increase in force will be obtained.

To digress briefly. This is how Bruce Lee, weighing in at most at 140 pounds. Could generate as much force as a heavyweight boxer! His speed was so exceptional that his light body mass did not matter.

So, if you weighed more than 140 pounds to effectively have the same powerful force as Bruce Lee, you would not have to have his blazing speed. If you weighed in at 200 pounds (providing this was all muscle and not fat). You could generate a substantial amount of force with a slower punch or kick than Bruce Lee. But all things being equal the highest velocity or speed is superior to any amount of body mass, and is always preferred way to train for speed.

## How to kill a king

To assassinate a king, president or VIP. Using the "poison hand" method. Requires more tact and a cool manner than adroit skill of striking directly. Indeed, you could just smile and offer a handshake with this person and unknown to them or the many bodyguards or agents surrounding the "mark". You have just effectively killed them!

Just as if you had used a violent method with physical attack or a close range pistol, or even long range sniper type rifle. The difference is you will have to make close contact with the 'mark' and have to remain calm while you make your exit and get as far away as possible.

Some important training you will need is to master your breath control. You do not want to alarm the people around your or the bodyguards/agents surrounding your 'mark'.

You will need to remain clam and think of pleasant things while you smile and look your 'mark' directly in the eyes. Knowing that you have made the kill is and can be very satisfying so you will not have to fake this when you have accomplished the task.

Practice while sitting breathing using your abdominal or diaphragmatic breathing. You do not want to breath with your chest heaving visibly giving an alert guard to see you are nervous. When you do this exercise imagine walking to the 'mark' and touching or shaking the hand. If you do this many times (I recommend at least 21 days before a 'mark' is taken out) by the time you take action it will be second nature and you will be home or sitting on a beach watching the NEWS with no connection to yourself and a contract well done.

If you still cannot remain calm during the approach, get some prescription "beta blocker" pills. Experiment with them as your reaction time will be cut down. But your eyes and hand will remain steady along with your heartbeat, and respiration.

Breathe with ease exercise

Inhale through the nose, expand your diaphragm.

Exhale out of your mouth slowly anc contract your abdominal area.

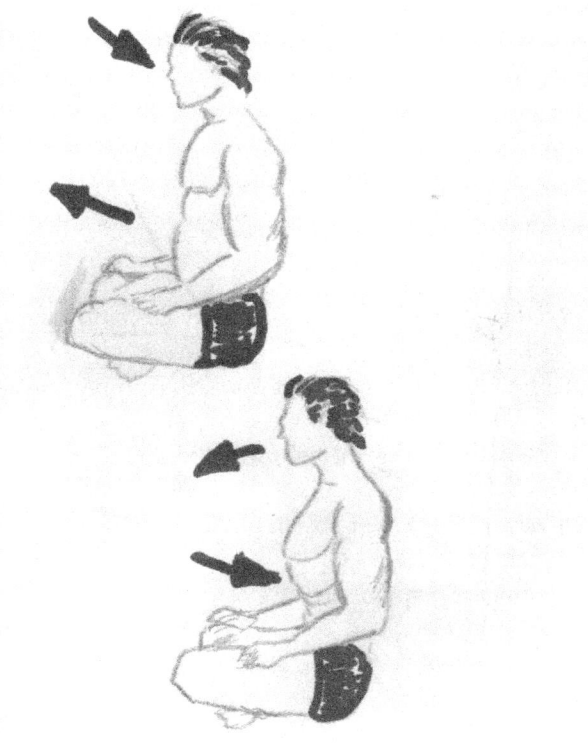

Next you must either have a special coating on your hand, or small pocket glued against your palm. That will protect yourself from contact with the toxic substance you will be inflecting upon the 'mark'.

If it is cold out you may be able to use gloves and gently touch the 'marks' skin on the wrist on the inside, or pose with the 'mark' for a photo and gently touch them on the neck or any exposed area of skin.

Some types of special glue applied on the inside of your hand when allowed to dry can make an effective barrier to protect yourself, or apply a layer of plastic wrap glued over the palm. In the ancient days one would train and become immune to the effects of the chosen poison and always have a small amount imbedded into the fingers or palm because of years of training. Many time toxic herbs or combination of them were used.

Now in this modern era, you have the choice to obtain some rather dangerous substances that will in effect do your work for you! All you have to do is deliver the 'bad news' to your 'mark'.

To be thorough, the other methods of delivery are equally as good. But can allow you to be discovered and that is that last thing you want happen.

Certain substances are very lethal and a small squirt gun or tube in your sleeve directed at the 'marks' face is all that would be needed. Even a coffee, or other beverage cup thrown at (or made to look like an accidental spill) on the "mark". The one advantage using this method is that you can have a few feet of distance between you and the mark.

One of the most lethal that can be used with this slight distance methods for delivery is; Prussic acid-(also called 'hydrocyanic acid' is so lethal that just a drop will kill a man within a minute and he will go down in seconds. A squirt gun shot to the face will effectively cancel his account. Or a splash into the 'marks' face render him dead.

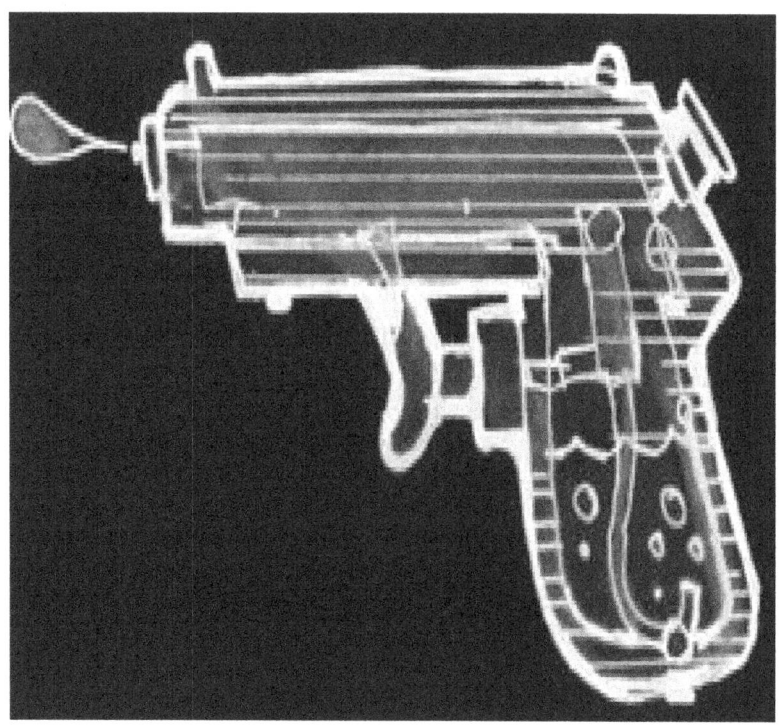

Another advantage of a basic squirt gun (let alone the new power pump ones) is the ease at which you can pass into Federal Buildings, and get on any aircraft because the metal detectors will not be able to seek out your plastic lethal weapon. Indeed, once onboard the aircraft you would have everyone effectively at your mercy. Or if your "mark" is in a public place at a civic function, state or county fair, etc. Hand the squirt gun to a kid along with $20 and tell him you dare him to shoot that guy in the face when he comes by shaking hands.

Another method of killing the 'mark' is poison by ingestion. This is a sure way unless the 'mark' is tipped off, to kill them.
The following dosages and poisons can be either dropped into the 'marks' drink or pre made into the food that they are consuming.
One advantage of the pre-made food/candies etc. is you could send it to the 'mark' by mail or courier and they would not be able to track you down and you would be effectively out of the loop. However if you are doing this as a

contract killing. You would have to keep tabs on the 'mark' by NEWS or look in the local obituaries. This method is NOT 100% reliable and could result in the 'mark' getting away or killing the wrong target.

Make a batch of cupcakes mix the poison of your choice in with the batter and make sure to use a sweet white or regular chocolate frosting. The "mark" will take at least on maybe two bites before dropping like a sack of potatoes. The following poisons are effective for this type of assassination.

1) Arsenic- A lethal dose is only 0.1 grams to 0.5 grams.

2) Ethylene glycol- This chemical is in most anti-freeze. It is sweet tasting and mixes well with cocktails. The chemical has the effect of shutting down the organs of the body-kidney's in particular are very painful way to die.

3) Nicotine- It will kill within 15-20 minutes after ingestion. Just a few drops will provide a lethal dose. It is common and available all over the world. The great thing about this toxic poison is the 'mark' will just appear to be intoxicated. It is great to put the nicotine drops in a glass of wine or other mixed drink and watch the 'mark' expire.

4) Potassium cyanide- If you can obtain this toxic substance. It will make your targeted 'mark' get his contract fulfilled so much easier. Just a few grains in a drink or mixed in a meal or sprinkled over a hamburger will do the trick. The amount of 437 grains to an ounce, and 16 grains to a gram indicate the effective lethal dose is very minute. It has hardly any taste and will kill within a matter of seconds to minutes depending on the amount and contents of the 'marks' stomach.

5) Dimethylmercury- is one of the most toxic substances known to man. Dimethylmercury is a heavy, clear liquid with many lethal properties. It evaporates readily, and is deadly if inhaled.
Less than a drop of it on your skin is a death sentence...but you won't die right away, You will die slowly, over months, as it eats away at the myelin sheath around your brain cells, slowly short-circuiting and eventually completely destroying your brain. It penetrates the skin readily, slipping easily through your pores and into your bloodstream, where it's transported

to your brain and begins its sinister work of destroying you from the inside. But that's not all. It gets worse, if you can imagine that.

Not only will less than a drop of it go right through your skin like a .50-caliber rifle bullet through tissue paper, it will go through latex, too. People have died by spilling it on their gloves in a glove box. One must be very careful when handling this toxic substance.

Once your toxic substance is chosen you should make sure you have a barrier between it and you. Test the deliver system and make sure it is flawless

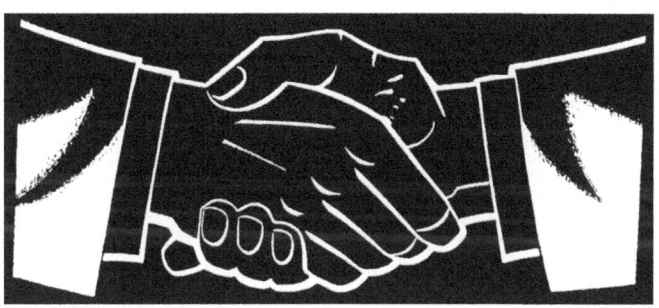

Care to shake hands?

## Cinnabar Palm

Cinnabar Palm is a "yin" or dark kung, or Black dragon Kung Fu. This is a most powerful "Palm". Once this is mastered it is a way to mortally wound without physical contact!

The master of this deadly art only has to gesture towards the enemy from a distance. The enemy will then fall immediately to the ground, as if struck by an unseen powerful force.

An enemy that has the mis-fortune of crossing such and adept will have only one to six days to live (at most).

The training for Cinnabar Palm, takes at least seven to ten years of non-stop disciplined training.

The training begins with a container (a shallow one is best) filled almost to the top with sand. The disciple should scoop up the sand and crush it between the palms and fingers. Letting it fall back into the container, attempt to cause the sand to move (only after preforming the first part of the exercise one hundred to three hundred times).

Attempt to now move the sand by passing the palms (Loa kun). Use your will (wei) to direct your ch'i (jing) out threw the "lao kun" chakra in both palms. Like the wind moves the sand in a dessert. At first you may see the sand only begin to be pressed down where your palms pass over. This is very good. Eventually you will be able to make the sand shift back and forth.

As you improve and increase your dark power. Replace the sand with gravel or small pebbles. When you can pass your open palms over the small rocks and make them shift and move. You have already become a lethal weapon. At this point if you wish to proceed further, replace the gravel with iron fillings and scoop up and crush it between your palms as you once did with the sand in the beginning.  Exercise this power everyday, and once per week take two paces back, while preforming this. Do this until you are now approximately

 twenty feet away from the container and still able to make it shift and move.

You now only have to wave your open palm at an enemy and they will fall to the ground dead!

## The lying tiger

This is a "yang" or hard kung. Used to develop the strength and density of the bones and muscles, primarily in the fingers and toes. The exercise has the appearance of the Western culture's basic 'push-up'.

This is how you first start with both palms down on the ground and only the toes touching the earth supporting the body. However, unlike the basic push-up, you will hold this position static and practice breath control.

Eventually work up to holding this position for thirty minutes. After one to two years. Start doing this on your fists. After another on or two years start this time by using just two fingers and a thumb with both hands (the index, and middle finger, plus a thumb).

Now shift the weight from just foot on your toes to the other. After you feel strong in this position. Have a training partner sit on top of your back while you still hold this position. Your fingers, thumb, and toes are now extraordinarily strong and merely pushing or kicking an enemy could result in great harm to anyone .

## Clamping and locking fingers

Clamping fingers are a easily master kung to train all of the clamping strength into the fingers. The disciple with trained fingers can inflict major harm to an enemy or even death if applied to the vital points of the body.

No equipment is required for this training and it can be accomplished anywhere. Stretch out the index and middle finger of the hand. Then one by one flex the thumb until it touches the tip of the finger's. Gradually increase the pressure being applied until you reach the pain threshold. Stop when this occurs. Then reduce the pressure and massage the finger tips with your thumb in a circular motion at first to the right and then reverse the direction for an equal amount of times. Make surer you incorporate proper breathing technique when you do this exercise. Exhale as you increase pressure inhale as you relax and switch fingers.

Locking fingers, is also increases your grip. When you grab or shake another person's hand you mst be very careful not to use the full power of your grasp. Otherwise you could break the person's hand or grabbing any body part will be ruptured.

Make sure when you exhale you guide the ch'i from your shoulders, to your arms, to the forearms and finally the hand and fingers. This will increase your strength immensely and is somewhat like a iron vise.

## The Heracles elbow

The Heracles elbow is used to violently to push away an enemy or objects downward or backward using the pointed end of the elbow joint.

The disciple should first lie on the ground with his back. Then use the two arms and the heels as sole support on the ground. Arms are bent at the elbows, the fists face forward palms up and legs are straight.

Repeated pressing back on the elbows raising the body up only with the heels of the body bearing some of the weight. Practiced controlled breathing and preform this exercise twice per day. Usually in the morning and in the evening before retiring.

The next step is to start using just one heel and one elbow. This will effectively double the weight and stress upon the desired elbows. Continue to preform this exercise for another year.

Then on the second year of training. Start to lie on a large flat rock surface. Preform the same build up in time and your task will be complete by the third year. If you use these now next to lethal elbows. The enemy will suffer greatly in pain and could sustain a deadly injury.

## The container kung

This kung is used to increase the hand strength in both grasping and crushing.

You will need a wooden dowel that you can attach a strong rope. The a clay pot with tow openings on either side. So you may pass the rope or cord through the holes and up to the wooden dowel.

Fill the clay pot container with sand. Leep the upper body erect stand in a "Ma bo" or horse stance. Now raise your arms out in front of yourself and gradually keep twisting the wooden dowel so the rope or cord wraps around the dowel. As you do this the container will rise to a spot very close to the wooden dowel. Then still holding the container at arms length slowly unroll the rope or cord in a reverse motion until it is once again resting on the ground.

After three months of this type pf training. Pour out the sand and add about half of the container with gravel. As you get stronger add two cups of gravel and eventually when it is full of gravel your forearms and hands will be very strong. Continue with this same container veen though after six months it should be full of gravel. Continue your training another two to three years. You will now have an amazing set of hands and forearms that will weld great power.

## Iron forearm kung

Iron forearm kung, is one of the fatser ways to develop an extraordinary power. First find a suitable tree close to where you live. Or a deeply buried round wooden post.

Stand in a "Mao bo" or horse riding stance. Everyday at the same time. For about 15-20 minutes, exhale out as you alternately slap your inner and outer forearms against it.

After you do this be sure to massage each of your forearms. In six months, your forearms will have become a lot harder to the touch and a lot stronger.

Now find a large rock or boulder, that does not have jagged or sharp edges.

Now at the same time of day as you were training before hitting the wooden post or tree. Start hitting the rock in the same manner striking the inner and outer part of the forearms. Breathing in when you pull away from the rock and exhaling as you strike the rock with your inner and out part of the forearms.

After six more months your forearms will now be like iron.

You can use them to strike or block any blow from an enemy. Addition grip strength can be obtained by following these exercises;

Get a bucket with sand in it. Take both hands and scoop up the sand. Press both hands together exhaling and pressing your palms together. Flexing your chest musclesand try to crush the sand into dust. Do this everyday, or every other day, until your forearms are pumped (engorged) with blood.

## Ancient Chinese Dim Mak chart dated 1241 AD

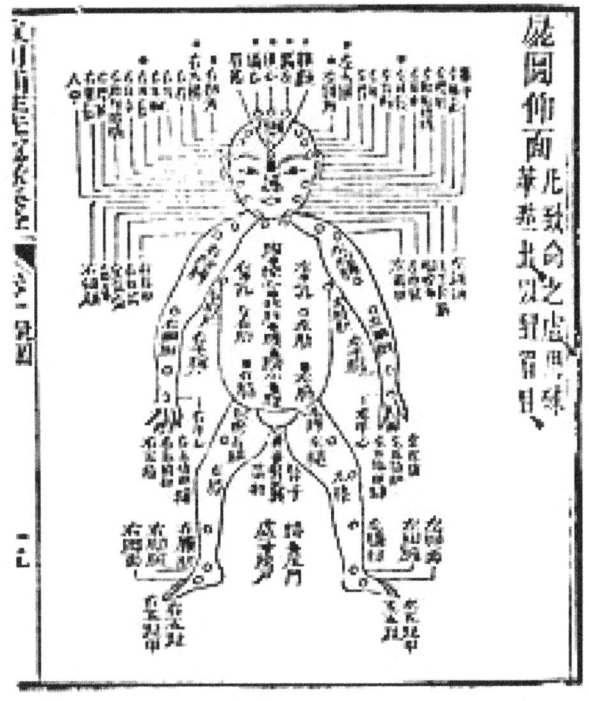

It is important to note that Chinese medicine does not view the organs in the same way as Western medicine does. Though the terminology is similar, the underlying concepts are very different. The Chinese cannon does not refer to an actual anatomical reality, but uses abstract concepts to define closely related body functions. Points on the large intestine meridian, for example, can be used to treat problems as diverse as arthritis, dry mouth, shoulder pain, and constipation. The Eastern organ meridian concept is based on thousands of years of observations of the external body, and not surgical exploration of the internal body.

In Eastern medicine there are five to six yin organs: heart, spleen, lung, kidney, pericardium, and liver. There are also six yang organs: large intestine, stomach, small intestine, bladder, triple warmer, and gall bladder. The yin and yang organ meridians are paired and generally represent similar bodily functions. So far, two methods of employing the Eastern meridian/pressure point system, acupuncture and acupressure, have been discussed, but there are many other effective ways of applying this knowledge.

Many Eastern healing methods make use of the concept of acting to "unblock the flow of Ch'i" in order to promote health and happiness. Jin Shin, for example, is a style which originated in Japan and involves a practitioner applying steady finger pressure on specific points for a minute or more. If done correctly, Jin Shin often induces a distinct feeling of well being and warmth in the person receiving the treatment. Due to the duration of contact, the practitioner can often feel the change in the quality of the energy passing through the points.

It may feel similar to a small electrical pulse. Another Japanese art, Shiatsu, which literally means finger (shi) pressure (atsu), involves rhythmically applying pressure with the thumbs to specified points for three to five seconds. The goal of shiatsu is to simulate the body's natural curative powers through stimulation of points on the meridian system thereby releasing excess lactic acid and carbon dioxide. The Zen Shiatsu practitioner uses a rhythmic pressure applied by varied hand positions. The point of the elbow or the knuckles will create acute pressure.

The palm of the hand has a broad target area, and is often less intense for the recipient. Tui Na, which means "push-grasp", originated in China some 2,000 years ago. It is a vigorous yet subtle style of massage of the soft tissue, specifically the muscles and tendons. Rapid hand movements over the body help improve the circulation and the movement of Ch'i. Thai Massage has been practiced for over 1,000 years.

It combines elements Japanese Zen Shiatsu with all these treatments are excellent for healing injuries and maintaining the strength of the martial arts practitioner, but knowledge of Ch'i flow, meridians and pressure points can be used offensively as well. Fighting arts with an emphasis on pressure point attacks such as "death touch," known in Chinese as Dim Mak, in Korean as Kuepso Chirigi, and in Japanese as Atemi, are believed to have evolved simultaneous to the healing arts.

Because of the highly dangerous and mystical quality of these skills, the techniques were jealously guarded. It was only in the late twentieth century that Westerners were able to understand and utilize these systems for attacking the body. Although it may seem unlikely that even an exceptionally well placed strike could instantly kill an opponent, the effectiveness of such a strike cannot be disputed.

Results can range from involuntary muscle responses and partial loss of motor functions (from damage to nerves serving muscles), to loss of conscious (for reasons which remain unclear, but hint at neural involvement).

Due to differences in body type and training, not all pressure point attacks will have the desired effect. Some people with naturally decreased sensitivity are seemingly unaffected by this sort of attack; other martial artists endure painful training procedures to deaden the susceptible nerves and pressure point regions. Boxers and kick-boxers are known to employ the latter strategy. People who are under the influence of powerful drugs or otherwise intoxicated may also be immune to some pressure point attacks. In a person with a taut, muscular body, the tsubo is pushed close to the surface, or close to the bone, and is therefore more easily triggered.

Consequently, very muscular individuals are generally more susceptible to pressure point attacks than people with a high body fat content. Assuming that you are not applying a "death touch" attack, a pressure point attack can actually be a less injurious form of defense:
By manipulating a body's weak points, it becomes possible to immobilize or restrain an attacker without causing serious or permanent injury.

Using this form of attack you can stun the body rather than seriously damage it. Another added benefit is that attacks on some points, like Stomach , which will be discussed later, inflict significant pain, but leave no permanent marks. Pressure point attacks can be just as effective when executed by smaller people and can be a tremendous advantage in defense against a much larger attacker.

Since the sensations are so intensely focused, and the point is often located just beneath the body's surface, it does not require much strength to make a big impression. The pain generated by a precise attack is generally of the shooting or radiating variety, and will often affect more than one part of the body. The sensation is immediate and difficult to withstand.

Striking There are several ways in which one might use pressure point knowledge during a fight. Because of the need for extreme accuracy, trying to hit a pressure point with a strike can be very difficult. There are a few points, which because of their convenient position and their standard degree of sensitivity, make excellent kicking and punching targets. These targets tend to be located on the lateral aspect, or perimeter, of the body. Gallbladder or "Wind Market" is a spot located on the outer thigh, midway between the hip and the knee. A well placed roundhouse or side kick to this point can cause instant and severe cramping in the leg. Large Intestine or "Outer Arm Bone" is a point that is located right below the insertion point of the deltoid muscle in the upper arm. A blow to this region can cause numbness, pain, or temporary loss of function in the arm. At the very least it will slow down future punches coming from that side!

Under the arm, in the center of the armpit is a very potent pressure point called "Extreme Spring" or Heart. It can be reached with a high side kick or front kick, assuming that the opponent's arm has been raised and is away from the body. Stomach or "Jaw Chariot" could also be called "K.O. Button," because a strong blow to the corner of the jaw where this point is located can cause the opponent to lose consciousness. There are many other pressure points located in the head that can be used to knock out an opponent. Unfortunately, as with all pressure point strikes, knockout strikes are very difficult to render effectively.

Wrestling Use of pressure point fighting in ground work, or newaza, is generally easier to perform than in a striking scenario. You are much closer to the target and therefore can attack the area with greater precision. You can also control the strength, depth and duration of the application. There are more pressure point target areas open to you during ground fighting as well. This form of attack is often used as a defensive maneuver in ground fighting, but it can also be wonderfully effective as an offensive strategy. Pressure point attacks can cause an opponent to release their hold momentarily, and thereby provide you the freedom to quickly move into a more advantageous position. Thumb to Gall Bladder. Heel Thrust to Spleen.

There are three pressure points on the lower body which are very vulnerable to attack during ground fighting. Gall Bladder or "Mountain Support" is at the bottom of the calf muscle bulge on the back of the leg. This tsubo is located along the sural nerve and is thought to be more sensitive in people who drink coffee. If one is pinned in a "four corner" position, it is possibly to disrupt the attack by digging your heel into this point on the attacker's leg. Spleen or "Sea of Blood" is a point located on the lower inner thigh at the bulge of the vastus medialis muscle. This point is most commonly attacked as a means to "pass the guard". A successful attack here causes considerable pain in most people, and a subsequent release of the leg lock that otherwise maintains the guard. Spleen or "Rushing Door", is a powerful target located a finger width above the inguinal crease. Continued pressure to the point can seriously disrupt the flow of blood through the body. It is often very sensitive, especially in males. This is an excellent point to attack if you are being pinned in a "full mount" or similar hold. When correctly applied, the attack causes the recipient to rapidly pull their hips away, thus enabling a defensive turnover.

"Extreme Spring" or Heart, located in the previous section on strikes, is another great spot to attack when you are trapped beneath your opponent. As demonstrated in below, a good strike there might cause the attacker to squirm away and release a mount, choke or hold, permitting escape.

There are two significant pressure points on the face that can be helpful in achieving kuzushi or off balancing for backward throws. Stomach, or "Facial Beauty", is located two finger widths from the side of the nose towards the ear, and directly below the cheekbone. The most effective application is to pinch the two points on either side of the nose with the index and middle finger, and then drive the head of the opponent backwards.

This breaks their balance and leaves them very susceptible to a reap. Another point nearby is Governing Vessel, or "Water Trough," which is located just beneath the nose. Applying a driving pressure to this point will have an immediate off balancing effect on most people. A palm heel strike to this tsubo will cause grievous harm to the recipient if bone fragments are driven up and into the braincase.

Joint Locks Pressure points can be used very effectively in a joint lock scenario. The hands are full of pain inducing points, not the least of which are the bases of the fingernails. Applying acute pressure to these areas causes searing pain, and will generally cause all but the most stubborn attackers to loosen their grip.

Thumb to Small Intestine, and Thumb to Large Intestine. In the webbing between the thumb and pointer finger lies one of the most well known and effective pressure points. It is known as Small Intestine or "Hoku." Lightly pressed it is said to relieve pain, particularly toothache, but pressed with serious intent it can cause a sharp pain that radiates throughout the hand. To bend an opponent's elbow, consider attacking Large Intestine or "Crooked Pond". This point is located on the top side of the elbow crease. A swift blow or a digging thumb will generally cause an attacker to retract the elbow towards the body. The wrist and forearm also have numerous points of pain that can be exploited in various wrist lock techniques.

Although you can try to find and trigger many of the points on your own body, the best way of learning is to find a partner willing to endure a little pain and prodding. An acupressure chart or diagram showing the primary points on the body will help, as those five thousand years of prior research will give you a head start in figuring out where to find hot spots. The Chinese have a system of locating points using bodily landmarks and a system of measurement based on finger widths. These measurements are called cun. For example Facial Beauty (Stomach), is typically described as being 2 cun from the base of the nose, towards the ear, beneath the ridge of the cheekbone. Acupressure points are generally found in joints, the splits between muscles and in the small grooves found in some bones. The surface area of the point can vary from the size of a small pebble to the size of a quarter. It is clearly more viable to use the larger pressure points as targets. The best way to find out whether or not you've hit upon an especially painful spot is to judge the reaction of your partner.

If their eyes flash and they quickly retract whatever part of their body your working on, you have found it! It is then wise to experiment and try to learn what exertion is required to achieve a desired effect.

If your intention is to heal, firm pressure may further block the Ch'i flowing through the tsubo and be counterproductive. A light but constant pressure will generally work best at relieving blocked Ch'i. The effected pressure point area will often become warm and may pulse under your fingers. The sensation is similar to moving sand. If you intend to cause pain, you will often have to apply considerable pressure, and your partner will most likely not permit you to hold the point long enough for you to feel any surface changes. As it has been done for ages, the way of trial and error is the best method of learning how to locate pressure points.

It is a tenet of some schools of martial arts that if you know how to break your training partners, you should also know how to put them back together. Up to now, I have discussed many specific ways of using pressure points to inflict pain and deter an opponent. The following series of simple Zen Shiatsu techniques and "G-Jo" acupressure.

These can be used at the end of a training session to restore energy balance and ease the pain in your training partners. To begin, have the partner sit cross-legged facing away from you as shown in Figure 10. Stand behind them with your knees lightly contacting their back. Take a good deep stance so that you can lean your weight in. Apply a firm and broad based pressure to their shoulders with the heels of your hands. Your arms should be straight and you should be using your body weight to press toward the center of their body. Rock gently from hand to hand, each time pressing into a slightly different area. To stretch out the shoulders place the hands on the far ends of both shoulders and press down on them evenly. Hold this pressure for ten seconds. Don't push down so hard that the person begins to fold beneath you.

It is very helpful to work key points, down the top of the back and over the shoulder blades as shown above. Use your thumbs to apply pressure sequentially to points one through five. Press firmly for five seconds at each point, working both sides of the back simultaneously from top to bottom.

When you have applied pressure to all five points, work your way back up in reverse along the same path. Next place the heels of your hands two finger widths from the base of the neck on the top of the shoulders. Press down towards the center of the body and hold at this spot for up to 30 seconds. This may be painful at first, but the pain should begin to abate as the point is held. Slowly knead the muscles on the top of the shoulders using a squeeze and pull rhythm.

A nice way to finish your massage session is to use some Tui Na techniques. A simple procedure is to clasp your hands loosely in a prayer position, as if you were holding an egg between them, and tap lightly and rapidly with the knife edge side of your hands against your partner's shoulders and back.

It is important that you do not use too consistent of a rhythm, as the body quickly adapts and becomes desensitized to the application of regular, rhythmic pressure. Instead, try to follow an irregular rhythm, perhaps by tapping to the melody of a song or nursery rhyme that you know. This brisk tapping will bring up the circulation and bring blood flow to the area.

It also helps with the flow of Ch'i in the region. Finish the session with hands flat, "sweeping" quickly, smoothly and effortlessly from the base of the neck to the edge of the shoulders.

Your partner or client will now feel relaxed and fresh. This can be repeated as many times as necessary or wanted.

## Glossary

Acupuncture- Chinese system of medicine and healing by the manipulation of needles on certain key points of the body, known as meridians.

Acupressure-The system of using pressure and manipulation of body parts to heal itself, G-jo acupressure is just one type of acupressure that can heal or stop pain without invasive needles.

Aikido - Japanese martial art invented by Morehei Ueshiba, involving internal and external harmony with nature, the techniques of this system are circular in movement, and heavy emphasis on development of "Ki" (Qi, or Ch'i life force).

Atemi - Japanese art of striking the vital points of the body. It is now used in jiu jitsu, but is illegal in judo contests.

Bandesh - Indian empty hand fighting technique used to defeat an armed assailant without killing him.

Bando - Burmese martial art involving numerous boxing methods. It is based upon twelve animals, which are the Boar, Bull, Cobra, Deer, Eagle, Monkey, Bird, Panther, Python, Scorpion, Tiger and Viper. It was introduced into the west by Dr. Maung Gyi in 1962. A very effective battlefield tested martial art that is very aggressive.

Bersilat - Martial art of Malaysia, derived from the Indonesian Pentjaklilat. It is also practiced in Java and Sumtra.

Binot - Ancient form of weaponless fighting found in India. This art is reputed to be more than 3,000 years old. The word means "something to protect", few the art is almost extinct today.

Blackbelt - Belt representing the fist significant rank in the martial arts training. Achieving this level of proficiency allows one to teach the art to others. In the Japanese ranking system it is known as Shodan.

Bo - Six or four foot staff used by Okinawans and Japanese for combat purposes.

Bohidharma - Indian holy man (who was a prince originally from his small village in southern India, also known as Ta'Mo and Daruma, credited with bringing zen Buddhism to china by introducing a series of exercises to the Shaolin temple, traditionally recognized as the origin of all Shaolin Kung Fu.

Bohokpai - Chinese system of kung fu based upon the mannerisms of the white crane.

Bokken - Solid wooden sword used for training purposes in kendo and other martial arts. In the hands of an expert it can deliver fatal blows.

Bokmeipai - White Eyebrow, style of kung fu, named after it's founder, Bok Mei. It is a very fast style of kung fu, which legend states to have been banned at the Shaolin temple after bok mie killed a fellow student in a fight.

Bushi- Japanese word meaning Martial Man to indicate a warrior who follows the code of Bushido, way of the warrior.

Bushido- Is a code of ethics, followed by the samurai, which stressed honor, loyalty, duty and obedience.

Cat stance - Stance used mainly in some karate styles, but also seen in Kung Fu. It places virtually all the body weight on the back leg. The name derives from it's resemblance to a cat about to pounce or spring.

Centerline - Basic theory of Wing Chun Kung Fu, in which students are taught to defend and attack imaginary line running down through the center of the body on which all vital organs are located (along with all yogic chakras).

Ch'an-(Chan) - Chinese reading of Zen, meaning Meditation. In India it is known as Dhyana.

Chang-Honyu- School of Taekwondo created by Choi Hong Hi. The name means Blue Cottage.

Chang San-Feng - Legendary martial arts master and great Taoist philosopher, credited with founding Tai Chi Chuan, one of the three internal systems of Chinese boxing.

Ch'i - Internal energy, the universal force which is harnessed through a series of special breathing exercises called Chi-Kung or Qi Gong. It brings it's users good health and physical strength. It's development is a prime requirement for practioners of Tai Chi and Hsing-1.

Ch'in-Na - Chinese art of seizing and grappling, identified as a type of wrestling but much more sophisticated. Great knowledge of anatomy is required by it's practioners before the techniques can be successfully applied.

Chien - Oldest known style of Tai Chi Chaun. It began in Chien Village and has 108 postures.

Chi Sao - Special exercise in Wing Chun Kung Fu for developing coordination and sensitivity in the arms. It is also very important for teaching correct elbow positioning and economy of motion. It is known in the west as Sticking Hands.

Choy Li Fut - Southern style of Chinese boxing based on the Shaolin Temple system. It was deviesed in 1836 by Chan Heung. If a very tall athletic person was to master this system it is almost impossible to defeat them.

Chuan-Fa - Chinese term meaning "Way of the Fist", correct term for Kung Fu.

Chudan - In Japanese Martial Arts the middle area or chest. In Karate this is one of the three target areas of the body.

Chungdan - Korean term to indicate the mid-section of the body, corresponding to the japanese Chudan.

Chunin - One of the three ranks in Ninjutsu, the middleman.

Crane - One of the five animal styles of Shaolin Kung Fu.

Daisensei- Title of respect, meaning Great Teacher, given only to a teacher of high rank.

Daisho - Matching set of the Japanese long and short swords, worn by all Samurai in the Tokugawa era.

Daito- Japanese long sword with a cutting edge, measuring more then 25 inches. It was used by the Samurai.

Daito-Ryu - Style of Aiki Jutsu from which it is said that aikido developed.

Dan - Japanese term for anyone who has achieved the rank of Black Belt or above. This term is not exclusive to the Martial Arts, but is used in many sports and Games.

Dim Mak - Fabled death touch, a delayed action strike aimed at an acupuncture meridian, able to cause death to a victim within hours or days of it's delivery.

Dit da jow - Special herbal ointment, the recipe of which is kept very secret, used to help pervent injury and severe brusing in almost all the Martial Arts.

Do - Japanese word for Path or Way, used at the end of the name of a martial art, as in Karate Do or Kendo.

Dojo - Training place or hall, used for the practice of Japanese Martial Arts.

Doshin-So - The founder of Shorinji Kempo, a martial art that is greatly influenced by Chinese system and is registered in Japan as a religious sect.

Dragon - One of the five animal styles praticed at Sholin. The mythical Dragon symbolizes the spirit and teaches agility and dynamic strength.

Drunken monkey - Style of Kung Fu based upon the antics fo Monkeys. Practioners stagger around as though intoxicated to fool their opponents. The style employs many ground and low techniques.

Elbow - Close quarter weapon used in almost all martial arts stystems. It is of particular interest to the Muay Thai fighters of Thailand.

Empty hand - Literal meaning of Karate in Japanese.

Escrima - Martial system fo the Philippines that employs sticks, swords and daggers. The term is spanish and means Skirmish. It's adepts are called Escrimadors.

Five ancestors - Five surviors who escaped during the sacking of the Shaolin Temple, credited with being the founders of the Triad societies.

Five animals- Five animals, The Crane, Dragon, Leopard, Tiger and Snake, whose movements were imitated in a system of fighting said to be the orgin of the Shaolin Systems.

Form - Series of choreographed movements in Kung Fu linking together various martial arts techniques, able to be performed as a solo exercise to aid the practioner in perfecting his techniuqe. The equivalent in Karate is called a Kata.

Fu Hsing- Chinese God of Happiness.

Fujow Pai - Tiger Claw, system of Kung Fu, developed at the Sholin Temple.

Full conatct - Form of Karate in which full power kicks are delivered at an opponent. Participants wear protective hand and foot equipment. The sport has grown rapidly in western countries in the last 25 years.

Gedan - Lower area of the body, from the wait downwards, in Japanese Martial Arts.

Genin - Lowest of three ranks in the Ninja Heiarchy. A Genin was the actual field agent, or Ninja, who performed assassinations.

Gi - Term used for traning uniform in Japanese Martial Arts. It is known as a Karate Gi in Karate and Judo Gi in Judo.

Gichin1 Funakoshi - Founder of the Shotokan style of Karate, and Okinawan Schoolmaster credited with introducing Karate into Japan in 1922.

Gojo-Kai - Offshoot of Goju-Ryu Karate, founded bye a student of Miyagi named Gogen Yamaguchi.

Gojo-Ryu - One of the major styles of Karate developed from Okinawan Nahae- It is a hard-soft system invented by Chojun Miyagi.

Gulat - Type of wrestling found in Jave, greatly influenced by Sumo Wrestling.

Gung Fu - Cantonese pronunciation of Kung Fu.

Guru - Referee at a Sumo wrestling match.

Hachidan - An 8th degree Black Belt, Hachi means Eight. In Japanese Martial Arts the title denotes a professor of the art.

Hadan - Taekwondo term for the ara of the body below the waist, equivalent ot the Japanese, Gedan.

Hakama - Long devided skirt,garment covering the legs and feet, used in Kendo, Aikdo and other Japanese Martial Arts. The long robe is said to mask the intricate footwork of the practioner, therefore making it difficult for an opponent to judge his movements.

Hapkido - Korean Martial Art involving many difficult kicks, but also utilizing locks and holds. It is somewhat similar to the Japanese Aikido.

Hara-Kiri - Japanese ritual suicide by disembowlment, known in Japan by it's proper name of Seppuku. It was the ultimate act of atinement by which a samurai warrior regained lost honor.

Harima - Tiger style of Penjak-Silat in Indonesia.

Heian- Name given tot he five basic katas in Karate. In some schools the Heian Katas are also known as Pinan Katas.

Hojo-Jutsu - Japanese art of binding or rope tying. First praticed by Samurai on the battlefield to detain prisioners for questioning. Adepts learn intricate methods of tying up a person with a cord.

Hombu- Headquarters of any Martial Art.

Hop Gar - Style of Kung Fu which became prominent during the Ching Dynasty of China. It was famous as the official martial art of the Manchu Emperors. Two distinct styles within the system were, White Crane and Law Horn. The style is also known bye the name Lama Kung Fu.

Horse stance - Basic stance, resembling that of a horse rider (Ma-Bo). In many oriental martial arts, especially Chinese Hung Gar and Japanese Karate, in the latter being known as Kiba Dachi.

Hsing -i - Chinese martial art created by the great warrior, Yueh Fei. It is sometimes referred to as Mind Form Boxing. The system is based upon the five Chinese elements.

Hung Gar - Style of Kung Fu stressing powerful hand techniques delivered from low stances. It is based on the movements of the Tiger and Crane and is one of the original five ancestor styles. Hung is the creator's anme and Gar means Family or System.

Hwarang Do - Way of the Flowering Manhood, a code of ethnics and a fighting system followed by the Samurai. The code was also followed in the Silla Kingdom of Korea. Today it's main advocate in the west is the grandmaster, Joo Bang Lee, who lives in the United States.

Hyung- Pattern of movements in Taekwondo, simular to a form in Kung Fu and a Kata in Karate.

Iai-Do - Japanese method of drawing a sword and re-sheathing it, a non combat art aimed at leading the prationer to intellectual and spiritual awareness.

Iai-Jitsu - Martial System from which Iaido was taken, a battlefield art which requires the practioner to draw his sword rapidly and strike to kill, and then replace it in it's scabbard.

I-Ching ( Book of Changes ) - An ancient book of Taoist divination principles. This book, reputed to be the oldest known book in the world, contains the philosophicas basis of Tai Chi Chaun, Pakua, and Hsing 1. It comprises 64 six line symbols, or hexagrams, each composed of two three line symbols, called

Trigrams. Together these symbols represent everything that exists in the universe.

Iga - Remote region of Japan famous as the home of the Ninja people.

Internal Systems- There are three internal styles of Kung Fu; Tai Chi, Pakua and Hsing 1. They each cultivate chi energy, and inherent power within all human beings, largely inexplicable to modern science, which can be unleashed to awesome effect.

Ippon - ippon is awarded for a technique which is judged as decisive, this is usually a move which connects cleanly, with good form and with little opportunity for the opponent to defend against it. Kicks to the head of an opponent or judo throws followed up with a strike to the downed opponent are particularly likely to be considered a winning ippon technique.

Iron body- Also called; "iron shirt", "gold bell cover". "Jinzhong zhao", is the repeated (over a long period time) beating and massage of the entire body. Gradually this is done with harder and denser objects (going from wood to metal) ending up striking and being struck with iron (caste iron is best). The result is that the human body will adapt and all tissue's become much more developed and conditioned to withstand any punch or kick. One that has been so conditioned is thought to be invincible.

Iron Palm - Lethal technique of Kung Fu, able to kill wit a single blow. the entire forearm must be conditioned over a period of several years before a student is able to attain any reasonable standard. This conditioning makes the adept's hand and arm like an iron bar.

Jeet Kune Do - Style of Kung Fu devised by the late Bruce Lee. It's name means "Way of the Intercepting Fist".

JKA - Japan Karate Association, founded in 1955. It is the largest karate association in the world. It's first chief instructor was the founder of Shotokan, Gichin Funakoshi.

Jki Jitsu- Japanese Martial Art based upon the exploitation of opponents strength against himself. The name means Soft or Flexable and the art contains both armed an unarmed techniques.

Jodan - In Japanese Martial Arts the top area of the body, from the shoulders upward.

Jonin - Highest rank in the Ninja Hierarchy. A Jonin received instructions directly from the lord.

Judo - Modern sporting form of Jiu Jitsu, developed by Dr. Jigoro Kano in 1882.

Judoka - One who practices Judo.

Jutsu - Japanese word meaning Skill or Art.

Kalaripayit - Indian system of martial training, of which two styles exsist, the Northern and Southern. It is chiefly practiced by the Tamils in the south and decedents of the Nayar warriors in the north. The word means Battlefield Training.

Kali - (or Ki-Ai)Super shout or yell in Japanese Martial Arts, emitted when applying a technique to add extra power and stun an opponent.

Kihon - Basic training moves, repeated many times in order to reach proficiency.

Ko Budo - Name referring to the ancient martial ways of the Japanese warrior.

Krabi-Krabbong - Twin swords combat system of Thailand, in which the martial artists fight at lighting speeds using two razor sharp short swords or a sword and a shield.

Kung Fu- A derivative of a Chinese term meaning "hard work" and "applied skills", now accepted by both westerners and orientals as a generic term for martial art skills.

Kup- In Taekwondo one of the eight grades of ranking before the Black Belt comparable to the Japanese KYU grade.

Kwoon- A training hall in Chinese; dojo-Japanese, dojang-Korean.

Kyokushin Kai - Japanese Karate System founded by the Korean born Mastau Oyama- It's name means "Way of Ultimate Truth". Oyama gained fame by fighting bulls barehanded. He still holds the world record for breaking the largest number of roofing tiles with one blow.

Kyudo - Way of the Bow, a Japanese Martial Art of archery which incorperated deep zen concepts. Great emphasis is placed upon the way in which one applies oneself during the ritual preparing the arrow for flight, actually hitting the target is of little importance.

Lao Tsu - Legendary sage in Chinese history, credited with founding the principles of Taoism.

Lathi - Indian Art of fighting with a Staff.

Lo Han - Name of any famous disciple of Buddha and also the name of the exercises that Bodhidharma taught to the monks at Shaolin when he found them in an emaciated condition. The method of training known as The 18 hands of the Lo Han is the basis of what we now know as Kung Fu.

Lung - Chinese word meaning Dragon.

Mabuni Kenwa - Creator of Shitoryu Kartate, who studied under the same Okinawan master called Hosu, as Funakoshi.

Makiwara - Striking post used to condition the hands and feet in Karate. Over a period of time the body part being trained in this manner will become much harder and denser than a person not trained this way.

Martial Arts - Term denoting the arts of war, taken from mars, the god of war. It now means a fighting discipline to promote combat proficiency.

Men - Protective face mask or helmet used in Kendo.

Moo Duk Kwan- Korean term for an academy for martial practice.

Mook Joong - Wooden dummy, shaped like a man, used for conditioning and training purposes in many hard, or external, styles of Kung Fu. It conditions the body much the same way as a "makiwara board"; notable Wing Chun and Hung Gar.

Muay Thai - Correct term for Thai Boxing.

Naginata - Japanese Halberd, or curved bladed spear, used in the martial way of Naginata-Do- This art was adopted by woman and is now a thriving combat sport in Japan. Although the spear tip has been replaced with a piece of bamboo for safety reasons.

Nahate - One of the three original styles of Okinawan Karate, named after the town of Naha, where it was first practiced.

Ninja - Secret society of highly trained assassins in old Japan, trained from birth to become expert in a vast number of martial skills.

Ninjutsu - Martial Art of the Ninja people. The original name was Shinobi.

Nunchaku - Two wooden batons linked by a short chain or cord to make an awesome weapon. Used originally as a rice flail, it is found in most cultures throughout Asia.

Okinawate- Collective term for the Okinawan schools of Karate. The name means Okinawa Hand.

Pa-Kau - Style of Kung Fu, based on circular movements with open palm strikes. It means Eight Trigrams and the concept comes from the classic Chinese treatise, the -Ching, or book of changes. The student constantly changes directions during an attack. Hence the art is sometimes known as Eight-Directions Palm Boxing.

Pentjak-Silat - Indonesian martial art of Muslim and Chinese origin. Many hundreds of styles exist.

Praying Mantis - Style of Kung Fu known in China as Ton Long. It is named after Wong Long, who invented the style after witnessing a fight between a grasshopper and a praying mantis.

Randori - In judo, free practice or sparring in which the techniques are not prescribed.

Rokushakubo - Okinawan six foot staff or pole made from oak or similar hardwood. Roku means six, Shaku means about a foot in length, and Bo means pole or staff.

Roundhouse kick - Kick used in virtually all the martial arts. It's circular path gives it extra power by generating a center force and it is on of the most powerful kicks in the martial artist's arsenal.

Ryu - School or Style in Japanese Martial Arts.

Sai - Three pronged, fork like weapon, once made of iron, now of steel. It resembles a short, blunt sword and is a single handed weapon used in pairs.

Samurai - Japanese feudal warrior. The word means one who serves. A samurai served as a military retainer to a lord and his shogun. A masterless samurai was known as a Ronin.

Sanchin - Breathing exercise of 20 movements used in Okinawan karate. It teaches a practitioner to tense his body and control his breathing during intense combat.

Savate - French system of foot fighting, correctly termed La Savate. It was the forerunner of traditional french boxing, called La Boxe Francaise, used in Paris by the underworld. It was influenced by Chinese Martial Arts.

Sensei - Japanese word for a Teacher or Instructor.

Shaolin - Temple in the Songshan mountains of northern China, where Kung Fu is said to have born.

Shinai - Bamboo sword made of four strips bound together, used in Kendo to replace the live blade.

Shinobi - Old term from shich the name Ninja derives.

Shinto - Japanese animistic religion, meaning Way of the Gods. It is based on ancestor worship.

Shorinji Kempo - Japanese Karate system founded by Doshin So, now deceased. is a Japanese martial art equivalent of Shaolin Kung fu. It was established in 1947 by Doshin So, a Japanese martial artist and former military intelligence agent.

Shorinji Kempo is a system of "self-defense and training" (goshin-rentan), "mental training" (seishin-shuyo) and "promoting health" (kenko-zoshin), whose training methods are based on the concept that "spirit and body are not separable" (shinshin-ichinyo) and that it is integral to "train both body and spirit" (kenzen ichinyo).

Through employing a well organized technical training schedule .................. (kamoku-hyo), Shorinji Kempo claims to help the practitioner "establish oneself" (jiko-kakuritsu) and to promote "mutual comfort" (jita-kyoraku'). The philosophy and techniques of Shorinji Kempo are outlined in their handbook.

Shotokan - School of Japanese Karate founded by Gichin Funakoshi. The name derives from Funakohsi's pen name Shoto. It is probably the most widely practiced style of Karate in the world.

Shuai Chiao - One of the earliest organized fighting systems in China, dating from c.700 BC. It was a form of wrestling, but with few throws. Today it is an official sport of the People's Republic of China.

Shuriken - Sharp pointed throwing stars, originally made of iron, a favorite weapon of the medieval Ninja and Taoist and Buddhist martial artists.

Sifu - Instructor in a Kung Fu style (there are over 360 styles od Kung Fu cataloged in China alone), corresponding to a Sensei in karate. The word means Father.

Sikaran- Martial Art found on the Philippine Island Luzon. It stresses kicks and leg techniques and resembles some Japanese Martial Arts.

Sil Lum Tao - Primary form in Wing Chun, meaning Little Idea or Little Imagination. The form teaches elbow positioning and the protection of the center line. It has no foot movements, only powerful arm motion and emphasis on the "chain of fists".

Sil Lum - Cantonese name for the Shaolin Temple.

Soo Bak- A Korean martial art that was combined with kung fu to produce the modern "Tae Kwon Do".

Sparring - Combat experience to give a martial arts student the opportunity to apply the techniques he or she has learned.

Sport combat - Martial arts competition in which combatants fight under combat rules in a ring or area. They wear protective gloves and foot pads. Techniques are scored and points are given. Actual combat is prohibited. Although some leeway is allowed.

Sumo - Ancient form of Japanese wrestling, steeped in religious aspects of Shintoism, contestants build themselves up to great weights in order to gain an advantage over their opponents. It is the forerunner of ju-jitsu.

Suntzu - Author of the Chinese Military Classic, The Art of War, believed by many to be the treatise upon which Ninjutsu is based.

Sweep - Technique in which catches the opponents foot or feet and unbalances them.

Tae Kwon Do - Korean style of empty hand combat very similar to karate. Great emphasis is placed upon delivering strikes with the feet and fists. This art was partly indigenous to Korea, being known as Tae Dyon in it's older version.

Tai Ch'i Chuan - One of the three internal systems of Kung Fu. Much value is placed upon it's therapeutic properties for the relief of stress and tension. It is intended to guide one into a state of peace and tranquility. The word means Grand Ultimate Fist. There is a deadly side to this art, but it is known by only a few instructors.

Tamashiwara - Japanese technique of using strikes with the body against materials such as wood, tiles, bricks and ice to test the power of a strike.

Tang soo do - "Way of the Tang Hand", a Korean Martial Art System very similar to Japanese Shotokan Karate. The style was developed in 1949 by Hwang Kee, who claimed to have derived it from the ancient Korean arts of T'ang Su and Subak.

Tao - Chinese term meaning Path or Way. Tao is an invisible force or energy, present in all things in the universe.

Ta Sheng Men - Monkey boxing, a form of kung fu that resembles the way monkeys fight (very fast and fierce).

Te - Okinawan term meaning hand which was combined with kung fu to produce karate.

Thai boxing - Same as Mauy Thai.

Thaing- General term of the Burmese Arts of Self Defense.

Tiger - One of the main animals in most styles of Kung Fu.

Tobok - Suit or Tunic worn by students of Taekwondo, consisting of a loose shirt and trousers tied in the middle with a sash or belt.

Ueshiba- Morihei Ueshiba, the founder of Aikido.

Vital points - Certain areas on the body which, when struck in a particular way, cause great pain or death.

Wado Ryu Karate - Way of Peace, style of Japanese Karate developed from Shotokan bye Hironori Ohtsuka.

Wazari- In competitive martial arts a score of half a point, awarded to the skillful execution of a technique.

White belt - The color of belt to a beginner in most Martial Arts.

Wing Chun- Chinese Martial Art invented by a woman named Yim Wing Chun. It's name means Beautiful Springtime. It is considered by many to be one of the most effective forms of Kung Fu in existence. the Fundamental premise of the style is economy of motion. Wing Chun greatly influenced Bruce Lee when he was formulating his own system of "Jeet Kune Do".

Wushu- Chinese term for the Military Arts, now use a generic name for the highly acrobatic martial arts of Mainland China.

Yang - In Chinese cosmetology the positive aspect of the universe relating to hardness, masculinity and light, one half of the Taoist view of the universe.

Yang Style - Style of Tai Chi, developed by Yang Lu Chan in the early part of the 19th century. It contains the original 13 Tai Chi postures.

Yin - In Chinese cosmology, the negative aspect of the universe, relating to emptiness, softness, darkness and female. Yin is represented as a black fish with a white eye in the famous Yin-Yang symbol.

Yokoaruki - Ninja secret walking techniques. The word means Walking Sideways. By employing such methods the Ninja did not reveal in which direction he or she was traveling, thus making it difficult for his enemies to track him.

Yokozuna - Grand Champion Rank of Sumo Wrestling, the highest of five ranks.

Yudansha - Kendoka who has achieved the rank of Black Belt or higher, alone permitted to wear an outfit of a uniform color.

Zanshin - State of mind cultivated in many Japanese Martial Arts. The student is supposed to become calm yet fully aware of his opponent's every movement.

Zen - Religious philosophy that claims that one can reach satori, or enlightenment, through meditation. Founded by the Indian Monk and Holy Man, Bodhidharma. Zen makes use of paradoxical poems called Koans to clear the mind of trivia and so reaches the meditative state required. In China, Zen is called Chan or Ch'an. Zen was much favored by the Japanese Samurai.

Zen Do Kai - The composite/ freestyle martial art system which originated in Australia by Richard Norton and Bob Jones when they left the Japanese Goju Kai karate dojo of Tino Ceberano in 1970. It was this Melbourne martial art that is excellent for bodyguards and vigilant security work to protect personal from harm.

Zhurkane - Ancient Persian (Iranian) term meaning "powerhouse". It refers to a system of highly specialized strength exercises and professes to be a *martial art dating back more than 3000 years to the court of the Darius.*

# Black Dragon Dojo Rules

Train your body and mind.
Be good and uphold your honour.
Respect your parents, and teacher.
Be honest and loyal to everyone.
Show compassion and mercy.
Defend yourself and other's as a last resort.

Made in the USA
Las Vegas, NV
02 April 2021